TRANSITIONS

MY LIFE JOURNEY FROM FRAGMENTED TO WHOLENESS

A Memoir

"Wilt thou be made whole?"

John 5:6 KJV

TRANSITIONS

MY LIFE JOURNEY FROM FRAGMENTED TO WHOLENESS

A Memoir

"Wilt thou be made whole?"

John 5:6 KJV

by

Robert C. Morris

Copyright © 2023 by Robert C. Morris

All rights reserved

This book is based on a true story. Names, characters, and some locations have been changed to protect the privacy of the people involved. The events described in this book are written from the author's perspective and, as such, are deemed a true representation from the author's point of view.

No part of this book may be reproduced in any form or by any means (electronic, mechanical, photocopying, recording, or otherwise) without prior written permission from the author.

ISBN 9798866305988

The scriptures in this publication are taken from the
King James Version of the Holy Bible in the Public Domain.

For information on the content of this book, please email:
Robert C Morris at morris_robert@myyahoo.com

Printed in the United States of America

Dedication i
A Note of Special Thanks ii
Introduction iii

Chapter One
    LOVE VS. LUST 1

Chapter Two
    PHOBIAS 8

Chapter Three
    WARFARE 17

Chapter Four
    VISIONS 30

Chapter Five
    FAITH CHALLENGES 41

Chapter Six
    FOLLOW THE LEADER 50

Chapter Seven
    FRACTURES 58

Chapter Eight
    A WAY OUT OF NO WAY 71

Chapter Nine
    FATAL ATTRACTION 81

Chapter Ten
    HEARTBREAK 89

Chapter Eleven
    DECISIONS 107

Chapter Twelve
    TRANSFORMATION 137

About the Author 143
   Appendix A 145
   Appendix B 146

Dedication

In loving memory of my mother, Onnie M. Morris, who taught me that despite your circumstances, with prayer and faith in God, you can fulfill your purpose in life.

She would constantly remind me that "where there is a will, there is a way."

"My Grace is sufficient for thee." ll Corinthians 12:9 KJV.

A Note of Special Thanks

To my sister, Mary A. Campbell, who has been the best friend and support in life that anyone could ever want. To my aunt, Sandra L. Johnson, who has encouraged and shared words of wisdom with me for the last 30 years. To the late Rev. Willie J. Sanders, whose anointed preaching led me to salvation through Jesus Christ. To Mercer Braun (deceased) and Sandra Braun, who helped me to develop a more intimate relationship with Christ.

To the late Rev. Milton A. Byrd, who took me under his wing and taught me patience and how to be a faithful Pastor. To Rev. Allen Thompson, Jr., Rev. Neva Lawson, Rev. Kevin Clark, and Elder Samuel Paraham for their spiritual guidance, invaluable counseling, and committed friendship. To my friend, Yolanda Dentley, and my niece, Linda Ellison, whose coaxing encouraged me to complete this book whenever I felt like giving up. To so many others who are not mentioned by name that have touched my life in a very special way. Love and thanks to you all.

Introduction

Webster's dictionary defines a transition as the process of changing from one state or condition to another. In life, we all transition in some areas naturally without effort, such as our change from childhood to adulthood. However, many of the changes we experience are sometimes unexpected, unwarranted, and even unnatural. Getting through these periods cannot only be difficult but confusing and downright painful.

It is natural for us to react most of the time with resistance to a transitional process because change challenges us to leave our comfort zone. Yet, I've come to realize that there are some transitions that we must go through in order to learn who we really are. These paths are often orchestrated by a higher power to lead us down a road to discovering our purpose in life and hopefully fulfilling it.

Many times, the reason people do not learn the skill of transitioning is because they have become imprisoned by their past or have developed a narrow vision of reality, which prevents them from seeing their true purpose. They go through life with a feeling of routine drudgery with no hope of escape. The fear of change can even render some powerless to see beyond the present and make void their desire for the next chapter in life.

Just as water cannot become steam without heat, we cannot fully transition without a motivating force that will bring about change to our current existence. Whether that force comes from within or from without, it must be there in order for a transition to take place.

It is only now, in my seventh decade of living, that my eyes have been fully opened to see how each of those transitional moments in my life had a specific purpose. These transitions do not occur haphazardly, as some would like to believe. Many times, they are sent our way as instruments that facilitate change. It is our individual reaction to these challenges that reveals who and what we are and determines what we shall become.

The purpose of this book is to encourage those who are despondent because they feel like life has not dealt them a fair hand. It is also to remind each and every individual who reads these words that your life does matter and that you are here on this earth for a specific purpose. No matter how difficult the struggle might be, always keep in mind that where there is a will, there is also a way. Come journey with me as I take you through what could have easily become a disastrous life that was made victorious through faith, prayer, and sheer determination.

Chapter One

LOVE VS. LUST

There was a mouth-watering aroma flowing throughout our house that afternoon as dinner simmered on the stove. The sound of the place settings being laid on the kitchen table could be heard upstairs in the room where my brother and I were playing some childhood games. We were separated by less than two years in age, and so naturally, sibling rivalry was a daily occurrence for us. After a few minutes of bickering, I decided to go to my own room to play by myself as I very often did. I was a loner who often preferred playing alone over playing with other children.

It was just weeks before my seventh birthday. I was excited about the possibility of having a birthday cake and what gifts I might receive. As I approached my room, I was beckoned from across the hall by Steven, who was an older resident in our household. "Come here; I want to show you something," he said as he slowly closed the door to his room behind us.

The next few minutes would change my life for decades.

Once inside the room, Steven pulled down my pants and began groping me. The molestation was simple in nature and over in minutes.

Robert C. Morris

I was frozen in shock and did not try to resist him. He made me promise that I would never tell anyone what had just happened. I left the room totally stunned and confused. As a six year old, I was unable to mentally process what had just happened. However, the emotional impact of that experience created a thirty-year transitional period within me where I struggled with sexual contact issues and intimacy. It left me in a place where I was emotionally unable to separate the emotion of love from the feelings of lust.

In the years to come, I found that love and lust had blended into one entity inside me with no wall of separation between them. Looking back, I do not understand why I did not cry or yell out in response to Steven's actions. Maybe it was the combination of fear and shame that silenced me. After all, my innocence had just been snatched away from me. However, even with Steven's stern warning for me to keep silent, it didn't stop me from going straight to my mother to tell her what had just happened.

Mom was a devoted mother who had lost her husband only five years earlier in a tragic car accident, and her life now revolved solely around raising her children. She was a serious thinker who was always concerned about the effects of what she allowed us to be exposed to. So, she hid the confrontation that she had with Steven from all of us, but needless to say, there was hell to pay in our household that evening. Soon thereafter, Steven was removed from our home. Mom's comforting talk helped me to push the incident from the forefront of my mind. Still, it would continue to emotionally impact my sub-conscience thinking for approximately the next thirty years.

Seven years later, when I was almost fourteen, I was still a loner and socially isolated. I had serious difficulty adjusting to new relationships and social interactions. I was a very shy teenager who was afraid of crowds and rejection. Many blamed my aloofness on shyness, but I think the emotional damage I had suffered caused me not to trust people and desire to spend a great deal of time alone. I used my time alone to read and absorb information about a variety of subjects. Mostly things of a

Transitions

legal or scientific nature. So, while many neighborhood kids seemed to be flowing over with gifts and talents of a physical nature, my biggest asset was my mind. Being a brainiac earned me many nicknames, such as "Mr. Know-It-All" and "Boy Genius", just to name a few.

I had been considered a child prodigy even in elementary school. My first grade teacher would take me to the principal's office and often to other classes to show off my spelling skills. My biggest accomplishment in first grade was being escorted by my teacher from class to class, showing them that I could spell:

H-i-p-p-o-p-o-t-a-m-u-s and **R-h-i-n-o-c-e-r-o-s**

However, being smart only contributed to resentment and jealousy from some of the other children. Many of them would resort to bullying and name-calling. This caused me to become more reclusive, and my seclusion made me even more socially awkward. Being alone represented protection from being mocked and/or bullied; it was a safe place. Somewhere between the ages of seven and fourteen, I developed a fear of crowds. The battle with this fear has been a lifelong one, which occasionally resurfaces today.

Mid-summer of my fourteenth year, while school was still out on summer break, I found myself extremely bored. I wanted to do more than just read, play card games, and watch repeat television shows. Many of the other young people spent their time swimming daily at the community pool. I could not swim and was extremely afraid of water. Because of my fear of water, I would not get near a swimming pool but would sometimes stand outside the fence around the pool and watch others having fun.

My fear was diagnosed by doctors as a condition called aquaphobia. Because of this disorder, I was excused from participating in pool classes throughout all of my school years. No one could ever determine how my severe fear of water came to be. My family theorizes that it was an emotional response to the shock of losing my father at an early age in a car accident in which he drowned. I was less than two years old when he died, but perhaps hearing stories about his death in my formative years could have traumatized me. Whatever the reason, this fear was another issue that I would have to live with and would take almost a lifetime to overcome. In the meantime, it would rob me of many enjoyable moments in life because things like fishing and swimming were just impossible for me to do.

Fortunately, that summer, the city government opened a community center designed for teenage boys to offer them some constructive activities while they were on summer break. Life in the inner city presented many challenges for teenagers with idle time and no resources. The community center was a large picture windowed converted grocery store. Peeping inside, I saw billiard tables, board games, weightlifting, and numerous competitive activities that sparked my interest.

The manager of the community center was a local scoutmaster named Carl. He was well-known in the neighborhood for promoting youth-oriented programs. Carl had convinced the Boy Scouts of America to sponsor a week-long camping trip for all the boys registered with his community center. The only cost to the neighborhood kids was a small registration fee. As much as I enjoyed the community center, I had absolutely no interest in Boy Scout camping. However, Carl was a longtime family friend and stopped by our house to sit down and explain the program to my mother. After a multitude of questions, she decided that it would be good for my younger brother and I to spend a week at Camp No-Be-Bo-Sco at Crystal Lake on Kittatinny Mountain in New Jersey. This is the same campsite where the movie Friday the 13th would later be filmed.

"This may be a great experience for you. It might help with your shyness and help you on your way to manhood," my mother said. If she could have only seen what was coming, she would have never consented.

I had suffered from separation anxiety many times in the past. I had a history of battles with homesickness any time I traveled away from home. I did not like leaving my comfort zone, and being away from home for an extended period of time made me miserable.

Transitions

My sister, younger brother, and I would take yearly summer trips to Missouri and Arkansas to visit my father's relatives. Weeks before we were scheduled to go, my bouts with anxiety would begin. My anxiety would result in me shutting down and isolating myself even further and many times crying both day and night. Many had said I would grow out of it. However, here I was, almost fourteen, and like a baby kangaroo hiding in his mother's pouch, I still had severe problems detaching myself from home.

Naturally, my anxiety started before we even got on the bus to go to Crystal Lake. My mother said to me, "Your brother will be there with you, so you will not be alone. Just give this thing a try."

However, once we arrived at the camp, I shut down emotionally. I tried repeatedly to find an excuse for them to let me go back home, but nothing seemed to work.

At camp, the scoutmaster assigned us tents. I was paired with a neighborhood boy named Allen. Allen was a quiet boy who was about two years older than me. I knew little about him except that he lived in the house around the corner from us and loved playing football.

Most of our days at camp were spent hiking and learning about nature. I found some of the hiking trips interesting because we learned a lot about nature. Nevertheless, I did not care for the fact that we were forced to march like soldiers and chant drill songs every single day. We were all assigned certain chores, and there was a time assigned for everything. A time to get up, a time to eat, a time for group meetings, a time for dinner, and a time to go to bed. Bedtime was the most difficult time because our tents were on the side of a mountain, openly exposed to the elements.

There was no running water or electricity at the tent site. If you needed to relieve yourself, you did it outside of the tent because the Main Hall was about a mile away through the woods. There was no TV or radio or even streetlights available, so we had to be in our tents and in bed by sunset, which was around 8:30 p.m. It was so dark outside that you could not see your own hand if you held it in front of your face.

Robert C. Morris

There was no door to lock, and once it was dark, you had no way of telling if anyone or anything was inside the tent with you. Having a tent mate was of some comfort because it gave a small sense of security while in total darkness. Sometimes, the light from the moon would provide just enough of a shadow to be able to see the outline of your bed. Mosquitoes and ants were a common thing in the night, but you just had to brush them off and try your best to sleep.

The darkness was unnerving, to say the least. I constantly thought, what if some wild animal climbed into our tent? How would we know when we can't even see our own feet at the foot of the bed? I think the dislike of the total darkness bothered us both so much that the first few nights, Allen and I would talk for hours until we fell asleep in order to deal with our fears.

It was about the fourth or fifth night just after I dozed off to sleep that I was awakened by what felt like a hand rubbing on my thigh. I thought that I was dreaming, and it took me a few seconds to realize what was really happening. Suddenly, it struck me that it was my tent mate Allen fondling me. I was frozen with fear, and as much as I wanted to move, I couldn't. I could feel my heart pounding so hard in my chest that it sounded like a bass drum beating in my ears. It felt as though I was dreaming, and I thought within myself that perhaps I would soon wake up. So many thoughts were running rapidly through my head.

Despite my fear, my body naturally responded to his groping. The groping turned into sexual frotting. Many thoughts rushed through my head as I lay there in shock and frozen with fear, pretending to be asleep. After a few minutes, it was all over, and I lay there feeling stunned and violated.

I wondered to myself if he really thought that I had actually slept through the whole thing. Somehow, I sensed that he knew that I was awake. I felt such embarrassment and shame because I did not resist. In some strange way, it was also sexually gratifying. He went quietly back to his cot without ever saying a word. Despite feeling violated, I was too scared to say anything to him or tell anyone else about what had happened.

This event only heightened my distrust of people and gave me more reason to not want to be alone with anyone. I became more reclusive and relived the incident over and over again in my mind. It only added to my confusion about sex and how to separate the emotion of love from the physical attraction of lust.

I somewhat understood what lust was from the unsolicited sexual encounters that I had experienced. However, the emotion of love had blended together within me with lust, and I could not grasp the concept. It was not until decades later, with the help of a therapist, that I was able to deal with my abuse. Therapy helped me to forgive my abusers. Once I was free from the guilt and shame, I was free to experience love unconditionally and without fear. For three entire decades, I had chosen to isolate my emotions and hide my pain instead of seeking God's help with this issue. Hence, this transition of learning to separate love from lust would take me over thirty years to work my way through.

There is no fear in love; but perfect love casteth out fear. 1 John 4:18

Chapter Two

PHOBIAS

My fear of water had gotten worse throughout my teen years. I had seen counselors and had signed up for swimming classes, but nothing seemed to help. Being near a body of water, even as small as a bathtub, made me panic, hyperventilate, and sometimes I would even pass out. As if I didn't have enough issues to deal with as an adolescent, this abnormal fear was growing, and I had no idea how to overcome it. Because of this fear, I could not go swimming, to water parks, go fishing, or even take a bath in the bathtub.

One Sunday, after getting home from church, my mother approached me and said, "I want you to join the church and get baptized." She was concerned that I would soon be eighteen and, if left to my choice, being baptized may never happen. My first thought was that with my history of enochlophobia, it would be difficult enough for me to walk down the church aisle in front of all those people to give the preacher my hand but to also get in a baptism pool with my fear of water was just impossible for me to do.

I tried to reason with her about how difficult it was for me to get baptized because my fear of water was debilitating. However, Mom was not the kind of person that you would want to present excuses to because she always had an answer on how it could get done. After all, her motto was "Where there is a will, there is a way."

Transitions

Mom took me to meet with the Pastor of our church, and he said he understood my problem. So, he decided that instead of baptizing me by himself, he would have two assistants in the pool with us to help relieve my fears. How would that help? I thought to myself. It doesn't matter how many people are in the pool, water is water! Between the two of them, they reassured me that I could get through the process, and I yielded to their urging.

Baptism day was one of the most nerve-racking times I had ever experienced. As I walked toward the baptism pool, my fears put me in a trance-like state. However, once I got into the pool, they baptized me so quickly that I barely had time to panic. I thought to myself that this just might be the beginning of my conquering this fear. Sadly, it did not get better, and my fear of water only worsened with time.

The older I got, the more socially awkward I became, and my shyness prevented me from making friends easily. I would spend most of my time in school alone. After school, I could be found alone in my bedroom. I found solace in listening to music because it would uplift my spirit and often feed my vivid imagination. Although I liked all kinds of music, I was partial to love songs that expressed the artist's inner emotions and their need to be loved. I spent night after night in my room singing along with those recordings, expressing my inner need to be loved. I longed for someone to emotionally capture me and change my life of reclusive behavior. I was almost grown, yet I had not even experienced puppy love in a relationship. So many unresolved emotional issues needed to be dealt with, and I had no idea how to address them. Then, out of nowhere, came an encounter I will never forget.

A girl named Hazel lived down the street about eight houses away. She was cute and kinda fast for her age and really knew how to speak her mind. These characteristics about her had, in some way, piqued my curiosity. I could not understand my attraction to her since we were basically polar opposites. I guess it is true that opposites do attract. I had taken a part-time job after school as a cashier at the corner store. Hazel would come in every day for her favorite bottle of soda.

Robert C. Morris

One day, Hazel struck up a conversation with me. We shared some stories about our families and our personal lives. "Do you like going to the movies?" She asked.

"Oh yes," I replied, and from there, we set our first date to go to the movies for that Saturday afternoon. Could it be that someone was really interested in me, for me? I thought that once she got to know me with all my hangups, this would be over quicker than it started. Little did I know that the courtship would evolve into an intimate relationship that would last off and on for seven years.

As we grew closer, I thought that I was in love, but I could not be sure because I still struggled with how to separate the emotion of love from lust. Looking back, I do believe that my attraction was a combination of both. Hazel did not help with the issue because of her hyper-sexual nature. I enjoyed her titillating nature, but I had difficulty understanding whether I felt love or lust. Did I want to be with her because I loved her or because I lusted after her? How do you commit to something that you do not understand? Besides that, we both had two totally different visions for our lives. Hazel dropped out of High School, and her dream was just to get married to get out of her mother's house.

This was a priority for her because her mother was an alcoholic and could sometimes be very abusive. Hazel seemingly had no dreams or aspirations beyond that point. On the other hand, my goal was to go to college, make plenty of money, and live very comfortably.

Another issue was that Hazel had developed a drinking problem. I'm not sure whether it was a generational genetic disorder or whether it was because she was predisposed to that behavior. This addiction was prevalent in most of her family. She was also a chain smoker who gave me my first cigarette. That cigarette turned into an addiction that lasted for the next eleven years of my life. Despite our differences, we continued to date each other for several years.

Once I graduated from high school, my mother said I needed to find a job to help out with the household expenses. "College can wait. Right now, we need money!" she said to me. So, from graduation day in June

Transitions

until late August, I would search every day, trying to find a full-time job. Most places rejected me because I was still only seventeen. "Come back when you're eighteen," many of them would say to me. I could not wait until my birthday in late fall, so I decided that I would change the birth date on my driver's license and officially make myself one year older.

Driver's licenses in those days were a simple printout on a piece of thick folded paper similar to a typewritten keypunch card. I was a very good artist and had won many awards in school for my drawings, so it was easy for me to erase the birth year date and pencil in a different digit onto my license to make myself a year older on paper.

In late August, I applied for a factory job and showed my doctored driver's license, and voila, I was hired! My official title was "Material Handler" for a light socket manufacturing company about 25 miles away from home.

The pay was a whopping $2.25 an hour. My job was to help unload trucks, stack shelves, and hand truck materials to assembly lines. A whopping ninety dollars a week was a decent beginner's salary in the 1970s. After all, gasoline was only about 36 cents a gallon back then.

The problem was I hated the job and had to work Monday through Friday from eight to five. This left me no time to go to school or even search for a different job. There was no internet or electronic applications in those days. You had to apply in person at the location where you wished to work. This had to be done at most places Monday through Friday during regular business hours.

After I turned eighteen, I wanted to look for another job and searched the want ads daily. My dislike for my current job was increasing by the day. It was mundane and required a lot of physical strength and very little brain power, which left me tired and bored every day. The position offered no paid sick or personal time off, and they were very strict about people calling out for the day. Vacation time was the first two weeks in July when the factory would completely shut down, and everyone was furloughed for that period. Employees who had worked at the company for a while had access to a vacation club. The employer would deduct a few dollars each payday from their paycheck and set it aside in a deferred compensation account until vacation time the following year. It was similar to a Christmas Club Account, except it offered no interest.

Including travel and unpaid lunchtime, the job kept me occupied from 7:00 a.m. until 6:00 p.m. five days a week. I hardly had time for myself and was beginning to feel trapped in what I knew was a dead-end job that I despised more and more each day. This created so much anxiety within me that I sometimes sat alone between boxes in the rear of the building at lunchtime. I would cry to release some of the pressure. I was miserable, and everyone around me could see it.

The anxiety turned into depression, and the depression made me even more anti-social. I had never been interested in drinking alcohol. Because of my fear of crowds and reclusive nature, I never went to parties or to nightclubs. So, week after week, month after month, I would lock myself inside my bedroom alone. Hazel would come by, and we would spend some time together. Still, if we wanted to be intimate, we had to do it in my car or somewhere else because I was still living in my mother's house, and there was no privacy. Besides that, my mother was very old-fashioned and would not allow us to be in my bedroom alone with the door locked.

When I went to Hazel's house to pick her up for a date, I could never stay or get comfortable because her family was always drinking and rowdy. So, we had very little space for privacy. I had always been a person of "right now." If I had an idea, I wanted to try it "right now." If something was due to me, I wanted it "right now." If my life was going to be different, I wanted it to change "right now." So naturally, after a year of depressing stagnation without some hope of achieving the things I had dreamed of, all kinds of negative thoughts ran through my head. Amazingly, even with my increasing depression, I constantly rejected the notion of suicide. Not to say that I didn't think about it from time to time, but that option was quickly dismissed. Primarily because my church

Transitions

had taught us that it was an unforgivable sin punishable by hell. Also, I had not figured out what was really there on the other side of this life.

As if I didn't have enough problems to contend with in my life, here comes another unexpected episode that scarred me deeply. It was a quiet Wednesday night. Everyone was sound asleep. My older siblings were now grown and had moved out of the house and living on their own. My mother, younger brother, and I were the only family living in our thirteen room house.

With plenty of space, we all had our own separate bedrooms and were in the habit of locking our bedroom doors at all times. This was a very good practice that kept down problems since Mom would rent rooms on the third level of our seven-bedroom row house for additional income. We desperately needed the money because my mother only received my father's survivor's pension. It had been cut dramatically since she no longer received benefits for my older siblings, who were now adults.

On that particular night, at approximately 2:00 a.m., I was awakened by a loud clanging noise that sounded like a fire engine bell coming from the stairway area of our hallway. I then heard the sound of a man's voice squealing like the siren of a fire truck. As I lay there trying to gather my senses, a feeling of panic and fear started to fill my body. I wasn't completely sure what was happening, but I could sense within me that whatever it was, it was not good. Then it came to me. The voice I heard was that of a man named Michael, one of the tenants who rented a room on the third floor.

Oh God, I thought. Michael has flipped the hell out! Michael was running through the halls up and down the stairs, pretending to be a fireman riding a fire truck. I could not understand why it was so quiet in the house. Other than the sound of Michael's voice in the halls, not even a creak of a floor in that old house could be heard. Where was my brother? Where is my mother? She had always been a light sleeper. Why was she not responding? My first thought was to call the police, but then I remembered that the only phone on the second floor of our home was in my mother's bedroom. Fortunately, my mother and I had adjoining bedrooms with a door that we kept locked for privacy reasons. I tapped lightly on the adjoining door with my ear pressed next to it. I heard my mother's voice on the other side of the door whispering softly, "The police are on the way. Just lay down and be very quiet."

I went back to my bed, trying to be obedient. Suddenly, a fist was pounding on the other side of my bedroom door. "Open up, it's the fire department!" Michael yelled out as he turned the doorknob and leaned his heavy body against my bedroom door.

I looked around the shadowy, dark room frantically for some kind of weapon. I could not find anything that brought me a sense of security. Michael was a big man, about six feet four and 280 pounds. I was six feet tall and weighed about 110 pounds, which was no match for him. As he banged and pushed against my door, I felt myself shaking. All I could think about was that I was going to die. I was stricken with a soul-piercing fear like I had never felt before.

I watched frightfully as cracks started to form in my white painted wooden door from the pressure of his weight against it. I ran back to the adjoining bedroom door and tapped again for Mom to open it. I knew Mom kept a gun in her room. At least I would feel safe in her bedroom. "Just be quiet. The police should be here any moment," she said again.

The hell with that, I thought to myself. If another crack forms in my door, I will kick that adjoining door down to get into her bedroom. The fear was so intense that I started hyperventilating and was about to lose consciousness. Suddenly, the doorbell sounded, followed by a sharp knock at the front door of our home.

The police had finally arrived. However, they could not get inside because the door was bolted with two locks and a deadbolt, and we were all trapped on the second floor inside our bedrooms. Just then, I heard the creaking of my mother's bedroom door opening. She had cautiously stepped into the hall with her .38 caliber revolver in her hand. Mom yelled into the stairwell, "Michael! Didn't you hear the doorbell? Open the front door!"

Transitions

"Yes, Ma'am," he replied as he walked quickly to open both the cylinder and the deadbolt locks on the front door.

I could hear my mother talking calmly from the second floor to the police as they entered. They began to ask Michael questions about why he was standing in the entrance foyer naked at approximately 2:00 a.m. with a bowl and a spoon in his hand.

Sadly, Michael could not remember anything or explain himself. The police explained that they could not evict him because he was a paying tenant. However, after hearing my mother's side of the story, they decided to take him to the hospital for a mental evaluation. He was released a few days later, and he stopped by our home to apologize and retrieve his belongings. After that day, we never heard from Michael again. What happened to cause him to behave that way? We will never know. However, the damage was done. Michael's one night of psychotic behavior had seared a permanent traumatic burn in my mind. This event created a phobia within me that I still struggle with over fifty years later. Even to this day, I find myself unable to sleep in a totally dark room. Also, the door to any room that I sleep in must be closed and securely locked.

Still, I occasionally have night terrors about some dark figure pushing open my bedroom door and trapping me inside of my bedroom. These dreams can sometimes be so vivid that I have actually called the police and family members for help before realizing that the experience was only a dream.

Sometimes, it would take a couple of heart-pounding minutes after waking up to separate my dream from reality. The trauma of that one night is still affecting me today. Will that ever change? Heaven only knows. My only comfort when faced with this fear lies in the promises of God's word.

Robert C. Morris

For God hath not given us the spirit of fear; but of power, and of love, and of a sound mind. 2 Timothy 1:7

Chapter Three

WARFARE

I was nearing my eighteenth birthday. Instead of being excited about the new freedoms acquired at the legal age of adulthood, I was battling depression. I felt so out of place and unable to smile and be happy about anything. My biggest hangup was that I felt life had dealt me a bad hand, and I grew less and less enthusiastic about living it.

How could I end up here?? I said to myself almost daily. I was an honor roll student and excelled throughout grade and junior high school. Many in school nicknamed me The Brain or Mr. Peabody because I was so knowledgeable and could present an answer for just about any question you could ask. In the ninth grade, I read and comprehended on a college level. The school aptitude test revealed that my IQ was 141, which is in the low genius range.

So how could I end up here?? Why haven't I chosen a career path that I could excel in with my gift of knowledge and retention of facts?? I am a great debater and have a unique ability to solve mysteries. My dream was to one day become a lawyer, but here I am, working for a little over two dollars an hour and afraid of the world. Why? Why? Why? I had no money for college and was denied financial aid because the rules said that my mother's income of $950 a month and my bring home pay of $296 a month exceeded the eligibility limit for a family of three to qualify for assistance. All I could think about was how I felt trapped in my circumstances with no way out.

The Church was an integral part of our family life. We were in church every Sunday morning, and neither my sibling nor I complained about going because we knew that it would not change my mother's mind about attending. Every Sunday after church, we were called to the kitchen to help prepare Sunday dinner. This practice helped to make pretty good cooks out of my siblings and myself.

Our church was a charismatic group with a weekly attendance of about 1,800 people. Being in the midst of that kind of crowd bothered me greatly, but as long as I sat down and did not have to say anything, I could handle it. However, having to walk through the crowd to use the restroom would almost throw me into a state of paranoia. I would sit week after week listening to the prayers and the sermons about God, but none of what I heard convinced me that God was real.

I wanted to believe in the existence of God, but the analytical side of me said that I needed more proof. You could say I had the "show me, I'm from Missouri" syndrome. Besides, I thought, if there really is a God, did he forget about me?? Why hasn't he answered my prayers?? I just needed more proof to validate what I believed at the time to be merely a theory created by older people to make them feel good about dying.

The beginning of my spiritual awakening started one Sunday night as I was soundly asleep. I woke up abruptly with a strange feeling that someone was watching me. How could someone get inside of my bedroom when my door is always locked? I thought to myself. I slowly opened my eyes and looked to my left and saw in my semi-dark room, about six feet away, a figure that resembled the shadow of a man. I instantly knew that this was not a good thing because my spirit was troubled, and I was laced with fear. I could not make out any physical details about this smoky image except for his eyes, which were clearly defined, and we stared at each other for about an entire minute.

My first thought was that my imagination was running wild, so I just pulled the covers up over my head. Shortly after, I could feel the left side of my bed being depressed, as if it was moving from the weight of someone getting into bed with me. I panicked and froze in place, unable to talk or move. My mind said, "Get up and turn on the lights," but as I tried to move, this "entity" grabbed me and held me tightly from behind. It was very strong, and its grip was immobilizing. I could feel its breath on the back of my neck. If I moved even a muscle, it would tighten its hold and produce a growling sound as if to say be still. I tried calling out for help, but not a single sound would come out of my mouth. All I could do was just lay there in fear until either the night was over or it decided to go away.

These nighttime visitations went on for months and happened several times a week. I tried keeping the nightstand light on all night, but that did not help. My mother and grandmother told me that the entity harassing me was something the old folks in the south referred to as a witch, and they had an old-time remedy for it. They had me place a Bible under my pillow with a dull knife on one side and a fork on the other. This remedy worked for a short while, but the visitations eventually returned. As the episodes continued, I became significantly sleep-deprived. Then, one night, as I lay in bed just about asleep, I could feel the presence of someone near me. I had developed the habit of sleeping with the covers over my head, so I slowly pulled the covers down from over my face, and there it was, standing beside the bed, staring right at me. Just before this particular incident, I had made up my mind that I would no longer be afraid and would confront it the next time it appeared. So, this time, instead of hiding under the covers, I got up on my knees and moved to the edge of the bed, looking it straight in the eyes with about twelve inches between us. I was terrified, but from somewhere within me came a strength I did not know I possessed.

A few seconds later, I opened my mouth to speak, and an uncontrollable utterance came out that spiritually cursed and bound this "thing" until it just vanished right before my eyes. I cannot remember exactly what I said, but I do remember the feeling of power that came upon me, enabling me to speak with such boldness and authority.

Robert C. Morris

Whatever took control of me that day was definitely from a supernatural source I had never experienced before.

I could never forget the hate and anger that I saw in the eyes of this evil being. However, I was now free from the reign of terror that it used to torment me for such a long time. I came to realize that the only power that it had over me was fear. If I could just be unafraid and fight, I would win the battle if this ever happened again. That night forever changed my thinking concerning good and evil, as well as God versus Satan. There is a battle going on, I thought to myself, and I have experienced the realness of it tonight firsthand.

Just when things appeared to be getting better, another challenge came to my peace of mind. Every so often, without notice, I would go into what was similar to a hypnotic trance with my eyes wide open. While in this trance, I would shut out everyone and everything around me only to see the events actively displayed inside the realm where I had unwillingly retreated.

Many around me called me a dreamer because they thought I suffered from a sleep disorder or was a serious daydreamer. However, these were not daydreams but powerful trances that would come upon me suddenly and without notice. I found myself visiting doctor after doctor, seeking advice on the cause and cure of this condition. Our family doctor said he believed the condition was a neurological disorder and referred me to a neurologist. The neurologist had me admitted to the hospital, where he and a psychiatrist ran a comprehensive series of tests.

After a week of tests and examinations, the conclusion was that I was probably suffering from a condition known as Petit Mal Seizures. Petit Mal Seizures are usually caused by abnormal electrical activity in the brain, which causes the person to go "absent" or "vacant" of attention for a short period of time. It usually lasts about 10-20 seconds. But in certain cases, it has been known to last much longer.

"Good news," the neurologist said, "This condition can be controlled with an anti-seizure medication. Also, because children are

Transitions

more susceptible to this disorder, it is very likely that this condition will resolve itself as you get older."

What a relief, I thought. I am not going crazy, but I have a known disorder that can be controlled and possibly resolved with time. Unfortunately, my joy was short-lived. Before I was released from the hospital, a psychiatrist stopped by to advise me that I should make a follow-up appointment with him for counseling. He also prescribed a medication called Deanol™, which he said would help regulate my behavior because, in his words, "You are too sensitive and a very high-strung young man."

The psychiatrist had a lengthy conversation with my mother concerning my prognosis. In his opinion, I would probably have a lot of difficulty adjusting to society because of my reclusive and neurotic tendencies. He told her to be prepared to have a dependent child for a long time and possibly a lifetime. "More than likely, he will never be able to hold down a job for very long because his attention disorder and reclusive nature will be a long-term problem," he told her.

I was neither trying to self-diagnose nor did I have a way to resolve my problem, but I did not accept the evaluation or recommendation coming from that psychiatrist. Needless to say, I never took the medication or made a follow-up appointment with him or any psychiatrist. I was determined that with my curious nature and analytical mind, I would find the solution to this problem on my own. However, instead of searching through books, I found myself praying to God for answers, even though my faith in God was still a little shaky.

During this time of seeking God and some answers, something peculiar began to happen. It seemed to come out of nowhere, but I developed this incredible desire to read and study the Bible. I had been in church all my life and attended Sunday School almost every Sunday. I was familiar with the basics about God and could quote some Bible verses, but this was a different desire. I was developing an intense thirst, almost like an obsession growing inside me, to know and understand more and more about the Word of God. I hungered for understanding in such a way that Bible Study became a daily preoccupation for me. It was like I was a sponge soaking up water.

I was barely eighteen years old, and my biggest interest was studying the Holy Scriptures. Others my age were out at the movies or concerts, and I was at home studying the Bible. During lunchtime at work, I would find myself a quiet place and sit alone in order to read and study. At home, after dinner, I would be off to my room to read and study. I had no idea at that time why I had such a fixation on the scriptures, but the thirst for understanding spiritual principles just seemed to consume me.

My preoccupation with the Bible caused me to miss out on many social activities and interactions with the few friends that I had. Of course, the lack of attention didn't sit well with Hazel, so she would often entice me with sex so that we could spend more time together. It wasn't that I didn't enjoy her company; it was just an overwhelming desire within me to gain more knowledge of the scriptures. I felt powerless to control that desire.

Once again, I struggled with finding a balance in life. Ultimately, I chose to spend my time in seclusion and meditation instead of social activities and social interaction. It's not that I didn't want to have a social life, but somehow, my day was not complete if I didn't have some study time set aside. In my insatiable thirst for Biblical knowledge, I also signed up for some correspondence Bible courses. Still, the deeper my understanding of the scriptures became, the more strange and unusual things would begin to happen to me. Each time I would sit down to study, I would sense the presence of someone nearby watching me. I often tried to ignore it or chalk it up to my imagination. However, many times, I would turn to my side and actually see someone standing across the room staring at me.

There were also times when I could actually feel the breath of someone breathing on the back of my neck, and when I turned around, there was no one there. The hardest thing for me was to make sense of all of this. First of all, I could not understand why I had become obsessed

Transitions

with Bible study. Secondly, I could not understand why there always seemed to be a distraction when I did try to study.

I did not know where all of this was leading, but I was laser-focused and refused to alter my course. Reading and studying was a slow and sometimes tedious process. Still, I could see that with a better understanding, my belief in God was slowly but surely increasing.

One evening, around study time, as I walked back from the bathroom to my bedroom, I heard a voice that sounded like a whisper calling my name. It was a different voice from any that I had ever heard before. I stopped and looked around. As I stood there, a message was telepathically transmitted into my mind. It said, "I want you to go and spread the Gospel."

My first reaction was to ask who was that, and you want me to do what? Was this God speaking to me? A few minutes later, as I was thinking about what I thought I had heard, I began to chuckle.

"I guess I have finally lost my mind because now I'm hearing voices," I said to myself. I believe that I was more concerned about actually hearing a voice than I was about the content of the message. The message stayed in my mind, but I did not take it seriously because to teach or preach the Gospel would require me to do something that, in my mind, was impossible for me to do, and that was to stand before people. Why would God want me to do something that I have no interest in or the ability to accomplish? Doesn't he know that I am an emotionally scarred loner hindered by uncontrollable phobias and have no interest in ministry? Heck, I thought, I'm still not 100% convinced that there really is a God.

Several months passed, and I had pushed that unusual encounter to the back of my mind when I heard the same voice again with the same message. This time, many questions arose in my mind that I could not answer. What does this mean? What should I do about it? How do I respond to it? Is this real, or is it just my imagination? These were a few of the questions that constantly ran through my mind.

Robert C. Morris

I decided to discuss the situation with my mother. She was always available to talk and a very good listener. I can remember her having such a serious look of concern on her face. After a lengthy discussion, she advised me to go and speak with our pastor about the situation. When I called the church, I was surprised to get on the pastor's calendar so quickly because Pastor Smith was such a busy man. He had only been with us a few short years and had become a popular evangelist as well as the leader of many Christian Organizations throughout the state. He was a tremendously gifted preacher and had been considered by many to be a preaching prodigy.

I grew increasingly anxious every minute I sat in the reception room, waiting for Pastor Smith to arrive. He was running a little late, which was no surprise since he was known for trying to accomplish seventy things in a sixty-minute hour. When Pastor Smith walked in a few minutes later, it was easy to see that he was preoccupied with many issues. About two minutes later, he invited me into his office. I was extremely nervous as I sat in front of his desk.

My mind raced as I thought about how to begin the conversation when he said, "I want you to be prayerful, and we will set up a date in the near future for the church to hear you.

I looked at him with astonishment and asked, "You know why I am here?"

His response was, "Yes, I do. You believe that you have received a call from God to preach the Gospel. So I want you to be prayerful, and we will set up a date soon to hear you. Is there something else on your mind that you want to talk about?"

"Ummm, no," I replied as I got up to leave the room. However, there was so much running through my head that I was unable to think clearly. How did he know what I came to discuss with him? Was this another sign or a confirmation of this calling that I did not understand? What in the world just happened here?

As I walked outside toward my car, I thought that maybe I should go back inside and tell him that this was all a big mistake. Oh God, I

Transitions

thought, what have I gotten myself into? I am so shy that I can barely speak above a whisper on a telephone. How would I ever be able to speak before an audience? I felt like I was drowning in a sea of misdirection brought on by my quest to understand who I am. In my mind, I said, "I do not want to do this! I can't do this!"

I was so unsure of myself and afraid to stand before people that I later called the church secretary and requested that my initial sermon date be postponed several times. For many months, I continued to make excuse after excuse, delaying what I had claimed to have received a Divine calling to do. It seemed like every week, someone was asking me why I had not gone forward with the process. When I ran out of excuses, I blamed others for the delay. I was really ashamed to admit the truth; I was petrified and resisting the call. I wanted to tell everyone that I had made a mistake, but I knew what I had heard was real. Therefore, I continued to find excuses to cover my fears, yet not deny my calling. Then, an idea came to me. If I were to join another church, all of this would simply go away, and the pressure would be off. Once again, I was mistaken.

I left my church and started attending the Jordan Baptist Church, less than a mile away. After attending for several months, I developed a friendly relationship with the Pastor of my new church. In a conversation one day, I confessed to him that I was running from what I believed to be a "calling." He said he already knew because he could see with a spiritual eye that I had been chosen. In one way, I felt trapped because I could not escape this "calling" thing. However, on the other hand, it brought a sense of confirmation to me that this thing was indeed real and not just my imagination. Not long after that, a date was set for my initial sermon, and I was accepted by the church and licensed as a Baptist Minister.

The Jordan Baptist congregation was plagued with strife and power struggles. This caused bickering and tensions that could be seen by everyone who attended that church. After witnessing a verbal battle in a church meeting that ended with threats and one congregant pointing a gun at another, I decided to leave and return to my home church.

The pastor at my home church was very understanding of why I had left in the first place. He accepted my papers from Jordan Baptist Church and welcomed me back. He inducted me into the ministerial staff of the church. Once I was active in my new position, calls started coming from many places, requesting me to preach at their church services. Being part of my church's ministerial staff and sitting in front of more than 1,000 congregants every Sunday had given me a lot of exposure. It wasn't long before I was asked to become a part of many organizations, including a position as an adviser for a group that ministered to young ladies on how to become mature Christian women. I was quite busy and very satisfied with the direction that things were going because the spiritual battles I faced previously had calmed down, or so I thought.

Wow, another great service, I thought as I left the church one Sunday. Suddenly, there is a hand on my shoulder and the voice of a weary mother speaking to me from behind. "Minister, I need your help. My son is sick and in the hospital, and I want you to come pray for him," she said.

"Did you speak to the Pastor?" I responded.

"No, I was spiritually led to you," she replied.

"What is wrong with him?" I asked.

"Well, they are saying that he's mentally ill, and they have him in a mental ward, but I don't believe this is a mental issue. It's a spiritual problem, and I believe you can help him," she said with tears in her eyes.

After asking several more questions, I finally agreed to visit and pray for the woman's son. I called my friend Samuel, an Episcopalian Priest, and asked him to accompany me and the young man's mother to the hospital. The hospital staff took the three of us to a special visitation room. A few minutes later, they brought in the young man. The staff left us, locking the door behind them. When I asked the mother why they locked the door, she replied, "Because they consider him an escape risk."

Transitions

The young man sat on the sofa between his mother and me. He was approximately twenty years old, stood about six foot two, and weighed about two hundred and twenty pounds. He was calm and greeted his mother with a hug, followed by the words, "I love you, Mommy."

"Abraham, these two ministers came to pray for you." Abraham nodded his head in acknowledging our presence but started to ramble and change the subject. He was so rattled by our presence that he became hyper, and it became difficult to understand what he was saying or where one sentence ended and the next one began.

Something inside me was battling with the same uneasiness that I remembered feeling when I confronted that unidentifiable presence that was standing in my bedroom many years before. It was as if another person was in the room with us. My mind kept racing, trying to relate that feeling to the current situation.

As my mind flipped through the pages of my experiences, it suddenly clicked that this was a perfect example of what I had learned in my studies about demonic possession. This boy is demonically possessed! I said inside of my head. Now what? Should I pray and lay hands on him? Do I leave and get some of my prayer partners to return with me? All these thoughts raced through my head as Abraham continued to ramble, jumping from one subject to another.

"Mommy, I've been reading the Bible. Got through several chapters today," he said as he picked up the Bible that his mother had laid on the table in front of him. Without a second thought, I opened my mouth and said to him in a sharp tone, "Abraham, mets le livre sur la table!" Which in French means *Abraham, put the book on the table!* I was testing him to see if he understood because it is believed that a demonic spirit can understand all languages.

He looked at me with a cleverness as if to say you almost caught me off guard. Then he stares me in the face and says, "Huh?."

Without breaking the stare, I repeated, "J'ai dit, mets le livre sur la table!" Suddenly, he slams the Bible down on the table with force and gives me a penetrating look of detestation. The evil spirit inside of him knew that I had sensed his presence.

"Who are you? What is your name?" I asked with a demanding tone.

"I am Abraham," he replied.

"Who are you? I command you in the name of Jesus Christ to tell me your name?" I said to him as I stood to my feet.

Once again, that authoritative force had taken control of me, and I was not the least bit afraid. Abraham's countenance had changed, and he began to speak slowly with a gravelly voice and a tone of force and said, "I know who Jesus is, but who are you? You think that you are somebody, but you're not sh**! "I was there when Jesus cast out demons, and that is what you're thinking. You think that you're going to cast me out? No, you're not! "Because you're not sh**. You are nothing! You have no power because you're nothing."

At that moment, I heard my Priest friend say, "Oh my gosh, what in the hell is going on here?" He started to back up slowly toward the locked door.

"Silence," I spurted out. "I bind you in the name of Jesus, the Son of the Living God. Be silent," I commanded. Abraham stared at me with contempt, but the spirit within him was bound by the command and unable to say another word. However, there was a low moaning sound coming from deep within him. Any doubt I might have had at the beginning of this confrontation left me, and something from deep within me had taken over both my words and actions.

As I moved closer, I began praying loudly and reading verses from the Holy Scriptures. I motioned for the priest to come and stand beside me and bring me the anointing oil we had brought with us. I anointed Abraham as he squirmed and grunted in tormented anguish. There was a will rising up within me to free this man from the power that had him bound, and I wasn't going to stop until he was free.

I had only been a witness in the past to spiritual warfare, and a couple of times, I had assisted in exorcisms. Now, I am leading the battle against

Transitions

an entrenched evil spirit with only the assistance of a freaked-out Episcopalian Priest and the young man's mother.

It was at this point that I realized that I was transitioning from a watcher to a warrior. All those years of being tormented by an evil presence had served to develop my spiritual awareness and increase my faith. I was not completely sure of the correct method to be used to drive this spirit out. However, the longer I confronted it, the more I was led by a voice from within about what to do next.

The battle to exorcise this young man took about an hour. When Abraham was finally free, he wept profusely with joy over once again being able to control his own faculties. His mother held his hand with tears in her eyes and did not seem surprised by all she had just witnessed. When things calmed down, she and her son expressed gratitude for the visit and the peace they were now experiencing.

As for me, I was so mentally and spiritually exhausted that it was difficult for me to even stand up. I requested that the priest help me to a different area of the facility where he could pray for me. I gave him my car keys so that he could drive me home. I was totally wiped out and unable to even drive. I understood what had happened but did not understand why I had become so involved in the situation. Little did I know that this was just preparation for things to come and a future transition.

Put on the whole armour of God, that ye may be able to stand against the wiles of the devil. Ephesians 6:11

Chapter Four

VISIONS

The church was considering ordaining me as a Reverend, which required a lot of study and preparation. I was in college all morning and worked Monday through Saturday evenings for a local newspaper company. The off-and-on relationship between Hazel and I had come to an end. We were still very fond of each other, but because Hazel was not a church-goer, she wasn't keen on the idea of me becoming a minister. It was hard to believe that not long before this time, we had considered marriage. Yet, we both could clearly see our obvious incompatibilities.

Among them was the fact that Hazel was a chain smoker who loved to drink, smoke weed, and dance. She had dropped out of school and had no desire to ever go back. I had picked up the habit of smoking cigarettes, but I despised drinking, drugs, and parties. All of these things really limited our common interests and our ability to spend and enjoy time together. Like Hazel, I despised school, but I believed it to be the vehicle for a better life, so I continued pushing my way through. Neither she nor anyone else would be able to change my mind about getting an education. So, we mutually agreed that our lives were on different paths and parted ways as friends.

Transitions

Once again, I was alone and not making sense of where life was taking me. I had grown tired of my job, my grades in school were starting to suffer, and I was becoming more and more reclusive. Wow! I thought to myself, maybe the psychiatrist was right. Am I doomed to wander from one thing to the next and never find a path to fulfillment and happiness in life? While pondering these things, it became clear to me that if I was ever going to become independent and find my way in life, I needed to find a place of my own and move out of my mother's house. I needed to feel like a grown-up. I needed to learn how to survive in the world and take care of myself.

Mom was not intrusive, but she did watch my every move like a mother hen watches her chick. She did not try to control me, but she had very strict house rules that often caused us to clash. One day, while driving along, I saw a relatively new apartment building with a new "For Lease" sign. This place would be perfect, I thought. It was new, in a nice neighborhood, and only fifteen minutes away from work. So, I made an appointment to see one of the apartments. During the middle of the showing, I told the manager, "I'll take it." I left the showing both scared and excited about having my own place. As I approached home, I wondered how I would break the news to my mother about finding my own place. Surprisingly, my mother seemed more excited than me that I would take that next step toward independence.

Moving day was bittersweet because I was excited about getting my own place. Still, I was sad about leaving my comfort zone. The move took only one trip because I only had my clothes and a portable stereo. I was able to load all of my belongings into my car. I also had an upright piano, which a friend loaded onto the back of his pickup truck and transported to my new place. So many questions kept running through my head. Am I doing the right thing? Will I be able to afford to live on my own? It was so exciting but also scary.

Well, here I am, I thought. There was no television to watch, no bed to sleep on, not even a kitchen table to sit at for dinner, but I was still excited about having my own place. For weeks, I ate take-out meals with plastic forks from local restaurants while sitting on the living room floor listening to music on an antiquated phonograph. I had no furniture, kitchenware, or even a mattress to sleep on. Of course, I would regularly stop by my mother's house to see what she had prepared for dinner. That was never a problem because she would always prepare enough for an army and expected me to stop by.

    I had worked hard at keeping a good credit rating. For about a year, I went on a shopping spree furnishing my apartment on credit. The more I bought, the more creditors would increase my credit limit. Being young and inexperienced, I foolishly fell for the bait, and before I knew it, I was over my head in debt. I found myself searching for a part-time job to help pay the bills. Finding a job was not very hard. There were plenty of employment opportunities around. The problem for me was how do I balance two jobs and school simultaneously?

    One afternoon, I was on my way to my mother's house. I ran into Ronald, her life insurance agent. After exchanging pleasantries, I told him I was looking for a part-time job. He said, "Why don't you come and work with me at the insurance company? They will help with your tuition and also send you to insurance school. You can make your own hours, and the pay is pretty good. You won't need that part-time job. Come in on Friday and put in an application. I will introduce you to our office manager."

    I was a nervous wreck on Friday as I walked into that insurance company office, not knowing what to expect. Ronald came out to the waiting room to greet me and handed me an application for employment to complete. "As soon as you're done, the manager would like to meet you," he said.

    The meeting turned into an interview, and I was offered a job as a sales representative with a pretty decent salary, a salary advance, and tuition assistance. It was an offer that I could not refuse. So, naturally, I accepted the position.

Transitions

Within a few months, I had sold so many insurance policies that my commissions had almost doubled my salary from my previous job. I could set my own hours and continue attending college, which was my number one priority. I was so excited that my life was moving in a positive direction. However, the celebration was short-lived. The office manager who had recently presented me with a trophy for the highest quarterly sales in the region suddenly decided that he needed to let me go because he despised my religious beliefs. He didn't speak with me directly but cowardly asked his assistant to fire me. The assistant told me the manager had commented, "If he talked more insurance and less Jesus, he would be an okay guy."

It was a devastating day for me because I had never been persecuted because of my religious beliefs. It was a stinging blow that hurt very deeply. Somehow, the word had gotten back to the office manager that I would spend time in the homes of some clients answering questions and discussing biblical principles. This was true and would often happen because many of my clients were also members of my church. Some would take my premium collection visit as an opportunity to ask questions. I was not an hourly employee, but I was paid by commission. So, if I spent all night on my route and did not sell, I would not get paid. Yet I was the highest-selling salesman in our insurance district that year. So how was that a problem? My schedule was never discussed with me. I had no warning or idea that this bothered him. It was a great lesson for me on the spiritual struggle of good versus evil and how when you do good, you will sometimes receive evil in return.

Well, here we go again: no job, no money, and uncertainty about school and the future. I refused to get involved with any illegal activity to pay the bills. I was able to collect unemployment benefits for a short time, but when it ran out, I found myself struggling with a feeling of hopelessness. I could not understand why life was so hard and why it kept dealing me so many setbacks.

After almost a year of job searching and filling out applications, I received a call from the telephone company concerning an application I had submitted years ago. "We need you to come in and take a placement test," the voice on the other end said.

"Tell me the date and time, and I will be there!" was my response.

The test was lengthy and difficult, but how badly could I have done? After all, I am a pretty smart guy who has never had any problems before passing a test, or so I thought. A few weeks later, I received a notice from the telephone company advising me that I had failed the test. What? How could that happen? I thought. I contacted the telephone company and got on the list for retesting. I did everything that I could to prepare for the second test. However, I was again notified that I had failed the second test.

The testing coordinator suggested that I apply for a lesser position; if I passed that test, at least I would have my foot in the door. I was reluctant to apply for the lesser position, but I took her advice and applied. I passed the test with flying colors. My test score was so high that I was placed in the top three applicants on the hiring list, meaning it wouldn't be long before I would be interviewed for a position. Within a month, I received a job offer, and it appeared that things were once again looking up, or so I thought.

One evening, I walked into my apartment with some take-out food and sat down at the table to eat my dinner. As I was transferring the food from the container to a plate, I heard a strange sound coming from the living room. It sounded like a cat scratching his claws across the walls. That's strange, I thought, since I didn't own a cat and my neighbor had no pets. When I heard it again, I walked into the next room to check it out. Perhaps some animal is trapped inside of the wall, I thought. However, that would be unlikely since I am on the third level. As I stood in the living room, it became clear that the sound I was hearing was on the surface of the wall and not inside of it. It was as if a giant hand was scraping its nails across the wall, creating a sound similar to fingernails on a blackboard. I was standing approximately five feet away, and the sound was very distinct, but nothing was visible there. Ten minutes or so later, it stopped just as suddenly as it began.

Transitions

A few nights later, as I was getting ready for bed, the same sound occurred on the same wall and lasted for about fifteen minutes. Soon after, the sound became almost a daily occurrence that would happen at almost the same time every evening. I began to suspect that this was not natural but might be some kind of supernatural manifestation. Is this really real, or is it just my imagination running away with me? I thought.

Night after night, I tried to rationalize this sound as perhaps being something created by my overactive imagination. However, the events of one specific night made it clear that it was very real. I had just arrived home in time to answer the ringing telephone. It was my aunt on the other end. We had been talking for about five minutes when the sounds began. "What is that noise? What are you doing?" she asked.

"You can hear that?" I responded.

"Of course, I can hear it," she replied.

"Auntie, that's the sound that comes out of my wall almost every evening I have been telling you about."

She yelled through the phone. "What? Oh my gosh, you need to get the hell out of there right now!"

Until then, no one else had heard this sound except me. With my aunt hearing it through the phone, it became clear that I was dealing with some unexplainable thing, but it was certainly not my imagination. I hurriedly left my apartment that evening. For the next few weeks, I slept at my mother's house while trying to figure out how to resolve this mysterious situation. I suspected it was something spiritual but was baffled by what it could be and how to approach it. Then, one day, I was led to seek the advice of a woman I worked with who was a devout Christian and wise in spiritual matters. I had great confidence in her and would visit her home for group bible study every week. I felt I could confide in her without fearing she would think I had a screw loose.

"Samantha, I need your advice on something," I said.

When I explained the problem, she looked at me and said, "My husband and I will be at your apartment on Saturday at 12:00 noon."

Robert C. Morris

Just as she had promised, Samantha and Martin arrived right on time and began praying and speaking in tongues as they walked through the door. It was very clear that they came seriously prepared for some kind of spiritual battle.

Samantha walked about ten feet inside the apartment when she quickly turned around as if someone had called her name. She was looking at the wall from which the noises had been coming. I had never told her which wall it was; before that day, neither of them had ever been to my apartment.

Samantha's eyes were laser-focused on a macrame hanging on the wall. "Where did you get that?" She asked.

"It was a gift from a female friend," I replied.

"Take it down and burn it right now!" She said in a firm voice.

I snatched it from the wall and took it outside, doused it with lighter fluid, and within minutes, the macrame was reduced to ashes. Samantha and her husband continued to read scriptures and pray throughout the apartment until the spiritual cleansing was complete.

There was now an overwhelming sense of peace in that place like I had never felt before. I sensed that I would be able to sleep in my own bed once again, and for that, I was eternally grateful to them. Of course, I still slept with a light on in every room. Some nights, I lay awake wondering why my life had so many spiritual challenges. I did not know it at the time, but these events were preparing me for a transition to a greater level of spiritual sensitivity and authority.

It was the year 1981. Many months had passed without any remarkable spiritual events. Then, one day, something really strange happened. Sitting at my desk at work, I had this very vivid vision. It came upon me suddenly without warning, and it was very unnerving. It was as if I had blinked, and suddenly, I was in a totally different location. A place that I had never been to before. I could see everything around me and hear every noise, every sound, and every voice. What I saw next was so disturbing that I felt myself trembling inside. I was frozen with fear to the point that I could not even speak a word.

I saw a man carrying a dead child, and he dropped that child into a field, got back into his vehicle, and drove away. The vision was so vivid that I noticed many details about the scene. I saw the color of the vehicle the man was driving. I noticed the position of the body and the color of the little boy's clothing. I was stricken with a fear like I had never felt before. Then, suddenly, in the blink of an eye, I was once again back at my workplace desk. It was as if I had been watching a movie on a television screen, and suddenly the screen went blank.

This vision troubled me so much that I could not focus on work. I decided to leave my job early that day. And because I didn't understand the vision, I did not immediately speak with anyone about it. What I saw was etched into my mind. I would have flashbacks of that vision frequently throughout the day.

Just a day or so later, while watching the news on TV, I heard a report about the body of a male child being found in a field in Atlanta, Georgia. The details were so eerily similar to what I had seen in the vision. Something inside of me went numb. I began to say to myself, "I was there. That's the vision that I saw!" But how could that be? I had never been to Atlanta, Georgia. I decided I really needed to talk with someone about this vision because it had left me bewildered.

The next night, I stopped by my mother's house for dinner and decided to speak with her about what I had experienced. I knew she would listen and not judge me or think I was making up the story. She understood that I was, as she put it, "different" and knew about all the other strange occurrences that I had been through. She often said to me with a little chuckle, "Well, you were always a little psychic." After hearing about the vision, she asked me a few questions and said, "Hmmm, I'm not sure what to tell you." We continued with our dinner and eventually changed the subject.

"Mom, it happened again. I had another vision," were the first words out of my mouth as I walked into her house a few days later.

Robert C. Morris

As I told her the details of what I had seen, she listened quietly until I was done and asked me some questions. This time, she had a whole lot of questions. "How did you get to see so much in a vision?" she asked inquiringly.

"It was more than a vision. I felt like I was actually there," I replied. The details were so graphic that I began to tear up as I recalled what I had seen. There was silence in the room for a few minutes. I wondered if my mother believed what I was telling her or if she thought I had finally lost it.

Then she broke the silence by saying, "Let me think about this a little," and gently sought to change the subject. Just a couple nights later, I went to Mom's again for dinner when the evening news came on with a special report from Atlanta. They had information on another child's murder. The details they released were precisely as I had described to her from my vision two days earlier. We sat there in silence, occasionally giving each other a look of disbelief as we listened to the reporter speak about findings at the scene that were fresh in our memories from our conversation two nights before.

"What should I do?" Do you think I should contact the police and tell them about the visions and the details of what I have seen?" I asked. I saw everything, and it might help their investigation, I said.

After taking a deep breath, Mom answered softly, "I think so, but you be very careful about what you say because you don't want them to think that you're a little Coo Coo," she added.

I called the Atlanta Police and spoke with a detective who listened to my story and said, "And you saw all this from six states away....amazing! Well, thank you for your help." I was courteously dismissed. I knew immediately that he did not believe me.

"Well, I did what I thought was right," I said.

Not long after that, I had another vision that was followed by another murder in Atlanta resembling the same details of my vision. I called the Atlanta Police again and was asked to leave a callback number. However, no one ever returned my call. I did not understand why I felt so

Transitions

compelled to even get involved. It was like a strange force was pushing me to share what I had seen with those who could stop these events from happening. Yet, in the back of my mind, I doubted that anyone would ever take me seriously. I sort of thought they would just dismiss me as some crackpot seeking attention.

After a couple more visions, I began feeling tormented by them. It became clear to me that I was supposed to be involved with assisting in the resolution of these horrific crimes. Why else would this be happening to me? I would ask myself over and over again. I am probably the most shy person on the planet and was uncomfortable speaking on the telephone. I knew that just speaking to those who believed only in scientific evidence and sharing my visions with them would make me look like some nutcase, but I felt compelled to do it.

The more the visions would come, the more I felt compelled to share information on what I had seen. Yet the more I tried, the more the officials ignored me. Then, one day, I saw the Atlanta Police Commissioner speaking on TV. Suddenly, it occurred to me that perhaps I should write directly to him, and maybe he would listen. When I wrote to the Police Commissioner, I delineated every detail about the murder scenes from my visions. Many of these details were never released by the police to the general public. I think the fact that I knew so much might have gotten his attention. When I think back, it makes me wonder why the FBI did not show up at my door to question me because the details that I described could have easily placed me in a suspicious light.

It was just a matter of days before I received a call from the Police Commissioner's Office thanking me for the information, which they said had been valuable to their investigation. The Commissioner's Office then sent me a letter with a contact number to call if I wished to share any further information. It wasn't long before I had another vision. I used the number to speak with a task force investigator. "I know his name! In the vision, I heard someone speaking with him, and they called him Wayne," I said nervously. "I saw the vehicle he was driving and can describe it. It was nighttime and dark outside, but I got a pretty good look at him," I said as I continued to ramble. The investigator listened attentively, asked a series of questions, and thanked me for the tips. (see Appendices A & B).

Shortly after that, the Atlanta Police arrested a man with the same name that I had given them and charged him with the murders. They considered the case closed because they had enough evidence to convict him. However, I believe from my visions that he did not act alone but had an accomplice who was never captured. I was a nervous wreck trying to understand why I had these visions and why I even got involved in such a serious matter as a murder investigation.

Even though I had done something good, I struggled for a long time with fears about my safety because of my involvement. What if his accomplice learned about my participation and came looking for me? Are the police now monitoring my activities because I know so much? All kinds of questions were constantly running through my mind. I began to start looking around corners and being suspicious of strangers. I wondered for some time if my life would ever be the same again.

It would take years for me to understand that this gift of visions is the norm for my life. The challenge for me has been to transition these visions into a useful tool that I can use to help others and to get insight into some things that would allow me to accomplish my purpose in life. Both of which would take time, effort, and a lot of prayers.

And your young men shall see visions, and your old men shall dream dreams: Acts 2:17

Chapter Five

FAITH CHALLENGES

I was now twenty five years of age and had barely gotten my feet wet in ministry. I was growing and absorbing things like a sponge in order to develop the spiritual gifts within me. My inquisitive nature and thirst for understanding of even everyday circumstances made me a natural-born thinker and seeker of knowledge. When it came to church, I naively believed that church-goers were different from everyone else. Just their supposed relationship with God, in my view, made them special, and I placed them in an exalted position. However, what I was about to witness not only changed my way of thinking about that matter, but it challenged my faith and stretched it to its limits.

One of the local Pastors was experiencing some divisions in his congregation that were being fueled by an ungodly faction of ministry leaders and lay people who were challenging his authority and his spiritual vision. Jordan Baptist was the same church that I had previously left because of the power struggles and strife that I had witnessed among certain church-goers. The Pastor and I had remained friends, and he asked me to come and meet with him. "I need your help; you are gifted, and you can see spiritually the things that I cannot see. I would like for you to come back for a little while and help me. I really need your support and your gift in my corner right now."

Robert C. Morris

How could I say no to someone who had been a great friend and a role model? So, with my Pastor's permission, I went back over to the Jordan Baptist Church to assist him in ministry. Almost immediately upon my return, I could see the spiritual warfare that was taking place in that church. Wow, I thought these people were behaving worse than most people I had seen on some street corners. They dressed up and claimed to be one thing, but their actions revealed the true evil that dwelled inside them. The worst part was that they seemed to have no remorse about their wicked behavior.

I watched as they would attack each other seemingly unprovoked and then say extremely hurtful things in an effort to express their anger. Prayer and worship were non-existent among them. Those who desired it left and went elsewhere to be a part of a church that believed in prayer and following the tenets of our faith. Many people there knew about my friendship with the Pastor, and I was considered by some troublemakers to be his advocate even though I had never confronted or expressed my opinion to any of them. As the divisive cliques grew stronger, they would make snide remarks to discourage me from attending their fellowship. As an immature Christian, I could feel my faith waning because I had begun to judge the nature of God by the ungodly actions of some of the people in the church. As time went by, it became easier for me to find reasons not to go to church than to find reasons to attend. Nothing was growing inside of me except anger and tensions from being in the midst of a group of bitter and ungodly people.

Despite the support of myself and a few others, the Pastor decided to resign, and the church congregation split. There was a small group that decided to leave along with the Pastor. Once again, the Pastor sat me down and said, "This is really why I wanted you here. You see, I always knew that I would have to leave, but I cannot lead the dissenters to form a new church because our regional organization would rebuke me and accuse me of causing this split intentionally. However, you are able to lead them and organize a new church from the group that left with me."

Transitions

What? I thought. Is he insane? I am barely twenty five years old and know nothing about organizing a church. Why I haven't even been ordained! The majority of the parishioners are senior citizens, and they barely know me. There were so many conflicting thoughts running through my mind, and yet, for some strange reason, as much as I wanted to say no, I did not reject his request.

The Pastor met with a few of the dissenting church leaders and told them about his vision of forming a new church and that I would be their lead person in ministry. He explained to them that once a new church was organized, he would be able to come back and join them in the capacity of Senior Pastor. Over the next two years, I worked diligently to get the group organized, recognized, and then sanctioned as a church by our Regional Baptist Association.

During that time, I helped them sponsor many fundraisers. I showed them ways to get donations from many local businesses and organizations to help with their building fund effort. My college major in Business Marketing really came in handy. The fundraisers produced enough money to purchase a building and some church furnishings. I had a vision one day, which led me to a building on the other side of town that I thought would be perfect for our congregation. The time had come to call back our pastor; however, the former Pastor of Jordan Baptist had left the area and accepted a call as Senior Pastor at another church. He strongly recommended that they ordain me and install me as their Interim Pastor, hinting that he would come back to them at a later date. The people accepted his recommendation, and with his help, a date was set for my ordination examination. I passed with a score of 98% and was ordained as a Baptist Minister.

After my ordination, it became evident that our former pastor was not coming back. A meeting date was set to confirm my calling as the permanent Senior Pastor of the newly founded Lakewood Baptist Church. A few days before that meeting, I had a vision of chaos erupting at the meeting. I knew from my past experiences with visions that this meant trouble was on the horizon. I wasn't sure what issue would cause the disruption, but I knew a divisive faction in the membership did not like me. They would more than likely be the sponsor of any chaos.

I could not understand how the same people who had left their previous church because of confusion were now about to start confusion in their new camp. I guess the same spirit that was in the others at Jordan Baptist was also lying dormant inside some of them. Now I would get to see their true colors.

I came to the meeting that night spiritually prepared to do battle. I had been fasting and praying that week for the strength to endure whatever challenge I would face. A really strange spirit in the place made me uncomfortable just to be there. I could feel the tension and knew that people had been talking about me because all eyes seemed to be looking in my direction. What have I done? What is wrong? I thought. Why am I feeling like prey ready to be pounced on by a predator? I could sense that it was not going to be a good meeting. I could feel the shift of spiritual balance in that place and braced myself for what was coming next. The gift of visions and my spiritual sensitivity had now evolved to the point that I could accurately predict when a satanic attack was about to take place.

My prediction proved true as the meeting started. The subject of choosing a Senior Pastor was now on the table. A small group of people did almost all of the talking. It was no coincidence that they were all related family members and their close friends. It was very obvious that they had agreed before the meeting on the complaints that they would air. "He's too young to be our Pastor," said one older man. His wife then shouts out, "He was our Pastor's handpicked successor and not our choice!" "He prays too long," said another family member. "He also preaches too long," said another.

They murmured and complained so long that others began to murmur about their murmuring. Once the bickering set in, there was an atmosphere of confusion, and a decision was made to adjourn the meeting and table the vote for a future time.

Transitions

I knew there had to be more to this than just those picayune issues. After all, I had been with them for over two years. We had plenty of time to get to know each other. I continued to smile while saying good night to everyone, but my spirit was deeply troubled. The coldness of people who professed to be emulators of a God of love had dealt a crippling blow to my faith. "When will I ever learn that church and helping others is just not worth it!" I said as I walked in dismay toward my car. I decided it was time to leave and return to my home church.

As hard as I tried, I wasn't very good at hiding my emotions and the dejection I felt. I am sure that it was very noticeable to everyone around me. The problem, as I saw it, was that I had allowed myself to become what people wanted me to be to them. For all intents and purposes, I did not have an identity of my own. I became somewhat of a chameleon to fit in and be liked by others. I also tried too hard to please people. Of course, my mistakes did not excuse their harsh and ungodly actions, but I do see how I contributed to the problem. Being young and inexperienced, I did not understand that being a people-pleaser can cripple you as a leader. Little did I know then that this flaw in my personality would later hurt me and rob me for decades of the ability to know myself and be true to who I am. For years, I mistakenly tried to be who people expected me to be and not who I was meant to be.

It is a true saying that no one can get to know who they really are until they learn to spend time alone getting to know themselves. Although I spent days, weeks, and even years alone, I did not take the time to examine the real me. I believe the transition to self-awareness took so long because I continued to allow people and positions to define me. For that reason, I would, for the next several decades, only see myself through someone else's eyes.

I finally reached the point of accepting that my work with Lakewood Baptist Church was no longer beneficial and reached out to discuss the matter with my former Pastor. "Leave them and come back home. They are a bunch of worldly and insatiable people," he said. So, with much regret, I gave my notice and returned to my home church feeling like a complete failure.

Over the next few years, I made a few new friends but spent very little time doing things with them. My preference was to be alone in study and meditation. Parties, social gatherings, and hanging out was just not my thing. I was degree-driven because I knew I had the capacity to achieve it. I believed that academic success would lead to wealth, and I thought that wealth would help me to find the happiness that was missing in my life. I had given up smoking and had no vices to fall back on except eating. I was always very thin with a great metabolism, so I could eat all day and night and never gain a single pound. It was not unusual for me to order a large pizza and a two-liter bottle of soda and devour it all by myself while watching a late-night movie.

I applied and landed a job at the largest newspaper company in town. The second shift assignment required me to work in the evening. This allowed me to go to college in the mornings. While working at the newspaper company, my desk was directly across from a guy named Joshua, and you could tell from looking at him that he loved to eat. Joshua had heard that I was a minister and one day decided to strike up a conversation with me about church. He was a very happy, family-oriented man who was a deacon in the Pentecostal Church.

Joshua was also a very talented singer and the leader of a community choir with members from almost every church and denomination in the city and the surrounding communities. It was impossible not to like Joshua because he was outgoing and jolly and never seemed to allow anything to bother him. Just out of nowhere, one day, he hollered across the office to me, "Do you sing?"

"No," I replied.

"Yeah, I didn't think so. I heard you in your car the other day, and it wasn't impressive," he chuckled. "I've noticed that you have great business skills, and my choir could use a business manager," Joshua said in a soliciting manner.

Transitions

"Who? Oh no, not me? No, I wouldn't be able to do that." I said in disinterest. "I have school and work and my own church duties. That's more than I can handle."

"Well, you don't have to work or be in school on Saturday night, so why don't you come on over to our church and watch our rehearsal at 6:00 before you make up your mind?" he insisted.

Typically, I would have called and made up an excuse for not being able to make it because I was so shy that I would avoid interacting with groups of people for any reason. But for some reason, I chose to go to that rehearsal this particular night. Everyone was so warm and welcoming. There was a time of prayer and supplication beforehand and a time of prayer after rehearsal. Boy, I thought, these people are serious about their faith. Joshua introduced me to everyone and told them that he wanted to nominate me to be their business manager in their election meeting.

Everyone seemed to like the idea and told me that they hoped I would accept the offer. I smiled and said I would consider it, but deep inside, I thought of every reason I could use to turn them down.

Over the next few months, every time there was a scheduled rehearsal, Joshua made it a point to verbally remind me, and I continued to attend. The time finally came for me to make a decision. I was unanimously drafted at the choir's election meeting as their business manager, and I accepted. I developed a great relationship with the choir and finally felt like a welcomed part of some group or organization. Joshua and I became good friends. Since we worked together and both liked to eat, we often spent time on our dinner break eating together.

For several years, our friendship grew closer. We shared time together praying and talking about church. Even after I left the Newspaper Company, our friendship remained intact, and I continued my duties working with the choir. Many times, when his wife did not cook, Joshua would call me to come join him on his dinner break. This was very convenient for us both since he was on the second shift with the newspaper company, and I had most evenings free.

Robert C. Morris

This friendship was such a change for me since I was used to doing almost everything alone, including eating meals. However, Joshua was just fun to be around, and he always brought laughter into any and every situation, including mealtimes. He even made our rehearsals fun and exciting. Hanging out with him was a refreshing change that had opened the door for me to overcome some of my reclusive tendencies.

It was a chilly Saturday morning in 1985, and I had morning classes to attend and errands to run. The Community Choir had a concert scheduled for that evening. Even though I did not sing with them, I tried to be present for every scheduled event to show my support and dedication to the group. My philosophy has always been that if you commit to a responsibility, you should give it your all.

I was just walking in from class and had dropped my books and briefcase on the sofa. There were two things on my mind: I was hungry and what I was going to wear to the concert. On my way home, I had picked up a cheese steak sandwich and was ready to devour it before it got cold when the phone rang. "Hello," I said, and a loud wailing voice on the other end kept saying, "Oh God, Oh God, he's gone!"

"What's going on, Johnny Lee? Who's gone?" I replied. "Joshua is gone," he said. "He passed away about an hour ago."

"Passed away? Passed away? Passed away?" I just kept repeating over and over again in shock.

"Yes," said Johnny Lee. "He was feeling sick, and I gave him a ride to the doctor. The doctor said he had the flu, but it wasn't the flu; it was his blood sugar that was out of control. Not knowing about his blood glucose level, we stopped on the way home to get some burgers and shakes, and his glucose shot up higher, and he passed out. By the time I got him to the hospital, his blood sugar level was around 1,100, and his heart stopped. They kept resuscitating him, but his heart kept stopping over and over again, and now. Oh God, Oh God, he's gone!"

"Johnny Lee, I have to call you back," was all I could say as a strange feeling came over me. It was an emotion that I could not ever remember feeling before. Many thoughts were running through my head. How

Transitions

could God let this happen? Why would he let this happen to such a good person? Why would he take away the only close friend that I had? I had officiated at many funerals and tried to sympathize with people before this time, but this was the first time I had personally experienced the loss of a close friend. The grief and the pain that I felt was almost paralyzing.

As strange as it may sound, the emotional trauma associated with losing a close male friend somehow tied into the emotions of losing my father at an early age. Although I was a child when my father passed away, the loss had damaged me emotionally to the point that I had subconsciously suffered from some kind of separation anxiety disorder. It is my belief that in life, all of our emotions are connected to one another. Each traumatic event either helps or detracts from our ability to cope with the next. I could not see it at the time because of the pain, but Joshua's death began a transitioning process that would help me cope with the next few chapters of my life.

Knowing this, that the trying of your faith worketh patience. James 1:3

Chapter Six

FOLLOW THE LEADER

It was now the summer of 1985. All of the associate ministers of our church were in a meeting with our Senior Pastor, who was also the moderator of our regional association of churches. As we reviewed some church procedures and asked questions, the Pastor said, "Oh, by the way, there is a church up in our northern district searching for a pastor. In the meantime, they need preachers to come and fill their pulpit on Sunday mornings. Since I am the moderator, I promised them that I would send some preachers to them to fill their pulpit for next month."

So, he randomly assigned each of us a Sunday, and his instructions were, "Go, preach the gospel, get your offering, and come on back home. Don't try to impress or campaign because I've already told them that you all have no experience, and for the most part, you're not ready to pastor a church."

When my Sunday came around, I was extremely nervous about my assignment. No matter how many times I had preached before, every time I stood before a congregation, I would still have a battle with nervousness. Until that point, I had only been to places familiar to me. This time was really different because I was going to a strange town and did not know anyone in that town or congregation. Being a perfectionist,

Transitions

my preparation for the date was excruciating and very time-consuming. Many nights, I would burn the midnight oil with very little sleep.

Because of my perfectionist nature, I strove very hard to ensure that every detail for my preaching date was well planned. I called ahead, got directions, and drew a map to aid in travel. I calculated the time it would take to pick up my family members and get to the church. I scripted every word of my sermon so that I would not be lost for words or make any grammatical mistakes. In my mind, there was just no way that I could mess this up. It was preparation to the highest degree.

However, that Sunday morning, I found myself running a few minutes behind schedule. I went flying up the highway, trying to make up some time. During the trip, I could feel myself getting more tense by the minute. The directions were easy to follow while on the highway, but it was navigating through that little town that became quite a challenge.

In those days, there was no GPS, MapQuest, Waze, or even cell phones, so the best directions were usually a map or word of mouth. I had always been directionally challenged and would often get lost in my own town. And now, even with all of my preparation, it looked like that same thing was about to happen to me again.

"I can't find Saint Paul Ave! Did anyone see Saint Paul Ave?" I yelled out. No one in the car had seen it, but everyone had a different suggestion about which way we should go to find it.

Ahhh, there's a phone booth, I thought. I'll call and ask someone at the church for directions. "Well, you're not that far away," said a pleasant female voice on the phone. "Just go back to North Walnut Avenue and follow it to Saint Paul and make a right turn, got it?"

"Yes, got it. Thank you, and I'll see you in a few minutes," I replied. As closely as I tried to follow her directions, I still could not find the church. Somehow, once again, I had made a wrong turn.

There's another phone booth, I thought as I pulled over to the curb. "You are almost right around the corner," said the woman on the phone with a chuckle in her voice. "Go back down Ellison Avenue until you get to the flashing light and make a right onto Chauncey Avenue. Follow it all the way to Saint Paul, and we are right there on the corner," she said. I was now forty five minutes late for service and so embarrassed that my thought was to just find my way to the highway and go back home.

How will they receive me, seeing that I am so late? Will I even be able to preach a sermon with all of the tension I'm feeling now? So many thoughts were rushing through my head. As much as I thought about going back home, my tenacious nature would not allow me to give up.

When we finally found the church, it was an awkward experience because they were about three minutes in the service from sermon time. I had to walk down the center aisle through the congregation to get to the pulpit. There wasn't even time for me to sit down and compose myself. I went straight from the door to the podium with everyone's eyes fixed on me. It was not only intimidating, but because of my discomfort with crowds, it became almost traumatic. These people will never invite me back again. I doubt that they even wanted to hear me today, were some of the thoughts that constantly ran through my mind.

I was embarrassed and so nervous that sweat was running down the back of my legs. I sweated so badly that the beads of sweat felt like bugs crawling down my calf. My body was trembling and my hands were shaking so much I could barely manage to turn the pages of my notes. I was very aware that everyone could see how extremely nervous I was, but I was unable to control or hide it.

Suddenly, I realized that the perfectionist in me had caused me to over-prepare on paper and the sermon was quite lengthy. I wanted to find a way to shorten my sermon because I could see that I was losing their attention. That added to the fear that was gripping me. However, due to my lack of experience, I did not know how to adjust the message. In my mind, the sermon delivery was jumbled and monotonous. I thought within myself that the sermon was dead on arrival. What kind of report will they give to my Pastor? I am so embarrassed that I can't wait to get to the highway to go back home. I waited weeks to hear some kind of feedback, but strangely, the church reported nothing to my pastor about that day.

Transitions

Four months later, I received a call from the Deacon Chairman of the West Road Baptist Church requesting that I come back and deliver a message for both Christmas and New Year's Sunday weekends. What? Don't they remember how I arrived an hour late? Don't they remember how I rambled and stumbled nervously through my notes?

"Sure, sir, let me get my pastor's approval, and I will be glad to worship with you on those dates," I told him.

With my pastor's approval, I returned to the small, struggling church to preach for them those two Sundays. I thought of it simply as an assignment that would give me some much-needed experience. It seemed to me that the people were more receptive this time and were paying careful attention to my every word. I had no idea they were considering me as a candidate for pastor.

After the benediction on the Sunday before New Year's Day, I was standing behind the pulpit and preparing to go and greet the people. When I heard a soft voice whisper in my right ear, "I'm going to place you here." It startled me because the closeness of the voice was as if someone had their mouth very close to my ear, but when I turned to look, there was no one within yards of me.

The sanctuary was filled with people talking and greeting each other. The sound of voices was everywhere. However, the voice I heard in my ear was quite different from the others. I not only heard it from the outside, but like sometimes in the past, I also heard it on the inside of me. As hard as I tried to dismiss it, those words kept resurfacing in my mind and stirring in my spirit.

I shared the whisper message with my family as we headed back down the highway. Most of my family found it amusing and made wisecracks that ranged from first you get lost and now you're hearing things. "You, a Pastor?" said one relative as she laughed hysterically. "You're too shy to answer the phone." "You have no experience in leading a church," were some of the comments I heard between the laughter on the long ride home. How I wish that they could see how serious I was. However, their laughter and jokes did not dissuade me from being sure of what I knew I had heard. I knew within me that it had to be some kind of message from God.

About four weeks had gone by. One evening, while checking my answering machine, I discovered a message from Deacon Smith of the West Road Baptist Church requesting that I call him. When I returned his call, he said, "The reason I called you is that at our church meeting, we elected you to be the pastor of our church. There were a few others that we had considered, but you are our choice. We will be sending you a confirmation letter soon. I'll get back with you soon so that we can set up a date for you to have an interview with the church board."

When I hung up the phone, I was overwhelmed by a barrage of emotions whirling inside me. How could this be? I never applied for that position. Why would they consider me? However, I instantly remembered the voice I had heard several weeks prior. So, did God orchestrate this? Is this something that I even want to do? What do I say? What do I do? My head was so filled with questions about this assignment that I would eat, sleep, and work with it on my mind every single day.

The interview with the West Road Baptist Church Board went well. However, a few congregants were dissatisfied with the church's election process. Despite the election and certified letter sent to me, a small dissenting faction kicked up enough dust to warrant another church meeting to discuss their election of me as their pastor. The real intention of the opposition was to void the previous election and start the whole process all over again. This group had someone else in mind and felt that if given an opportunity, they could change the election results and possibly get their candidate elected.

The meeting did not go as that group had hoped. I was elected a second time by a unanimous vote. To try to satisfy a small opposing minority, the Church Board sent me a second certified letter reconfirming my election, but this time stipulating that it was just for a one year probationary period. The one year stipulation was added to appease the dissenting few.

Transitions

The decision of the Church Board to change the results of the body's vote caused an uproar. A third meeting date was set to discuss and settle the matter once and for all. I was asked to sit in on the third meeting as Pastor-Elect. I chose to watch silently from the rear pew. I had a dream or perhaps a vision just a few nights earlier. In this vision, I saw the events that would take place in that upcoming meeting. I was told in the vision by that same soft voice that I heard months earlier to go and touch certain people in the congregation on their foreheads. I was obedient even though I did not know any of the people I touched. However, in this vision, when I touched them, they were instantly slain in the spirit. Even though I did not understand the meaning of the vision, it now gave me a strange sense of security about what was happening around me in the actual meeting.

As I sat in the meeting, I could actually recognize the faces of those that I had touched in the vision. Those I touched were hostile toward me, calling for a total election do-over. There was one argument after another, and nothing was being resolved. The meeting chairman acknowledged a woman in the congregation who requested to speak and gave her the microphone. She rebuked the Church Board for giving in to the pressure of a few and changing a bona fide decision by the church body. "Your letter putting probationary restrictions on our decision is illegal," she said vehemently.

She recommended that the head of the Church Board resign and the church vote that evening to re-certify their previous decision and make it final. The majority agreed. When it was time to vote, those who I had touched in my vision and were there to resist my election this time voted to re-certify it, and the vote to elect indefinitely was unanimous.

I was sitting there thinking that only God could have done this, and the pathway had been opened right before my eyes. But where is this path going? What is the purpose of all this? I cannot imagine what I could possibly be here to do, but I will be obedient and accept this assignment. Once I accepted the call, my transition from a follower to a leader began. This transition was a difficult process that started with so many obstacles, problems, and spiritual battles that I considered giving up almost every single week.

There was a sudden awakening within me of the enormous responsibility that had been placed upon my shoulders. I could no longer look to my leader for answers, but now many were looking to me for guidance. There was much to do because this was a special group with special needs who needed special attention. They had been hurt many times before by unscrupulous leaders, and many were afraid to trust again. Despite these issues, something was developing deep inside me that kept me motivated. I began to acquire a special love that affected me in a different way than I had ever experienced before. It not only motivated me to teach, guide, and protect them, but it also filled a deep void inside of myself.

I believe that inner void had been created by my desire to have children, yet I had none of my own. Not having children is something that I have regretted most of my adult life. Yet, in some way, the parishioners had become like my own children because they were dependent upon me for spiritual nurturing, protection, and guidance. I also learned from the leadership experience that without problems, you will never grow. Because no matter what some book or school may teach you about leadership, it is not the same as when you personally face the challenges head-on.

As time went by, the congregation grew. I began to transition into a more mature leader. Since I am a person who takes commitment and responsibility very seriously, I experienced a high level of stress trying to be everywhere for everyone and trying to resolve every little problem that presented itself. On an average day, I commuted 150 miles while also working a full-time job, administrating a church, and trying to complete my educational goals. If it sounds like a path to a stress-induced breakdown, believe me, it was. Still, each time I pushed myself to the edge, there was some supernatural power that intervened and kept me from falling off the cliff.

Transitions

All I could think about was how much this church needed a committed leader who had their best interest in mind. Someone who had a vision and that they could depend on and trust. It was obvious to me that I had developed a shepherd's heart and had the gift of prophetic visions. God worked many miraculous deeds within that congregation through me.

There was an instantaneous raising of a brain-dead young man from his coma that stands out in my mind. Then, there was a Sunday morning when the worship service turned into a healing service. The Spirit of God moved so mightily in that place that almost one-half of the congregation was slain in the spirit and miraculously healed of multiple diseases. Still, I could feel that something was coming down the pipes that would be the biggest challenge yet. They would need a solid leader with a vision to guide them as a congregation through that transitional period.

Where there is no vision, the people perish. Proverbs 20:18

Chapter Seven

FRACTURES

I had been overseeing the church for three years and had just landed a new and prestigious job. Things were going well for me from both a financial and spiritual perspective. Money was rolling in, I had accomplished my educational goals, and my life was changing fast. I traded my old clunker for a brand new luxury car. I could buy whatever I wanted to buy. I could eat whatever I wanted to eat, and I did not have to worry about how I would pay for things. Many days, I felt guilty for having such an abundance. I would constantly buy gifts and give money to charities and those I saw in need out of gratitude for my abundance.

Unfortunately, accomplishing my educational goals and holding positions of authority had caused me to start thinking too highly of myself. If anyone ever tells you that money and power don't change people, they are lying because it does, and it changed me. It did not make me mean or stingy. Still, there was an arrogant pride brewing inside of me that would occasionally surface. Several people close to me could see it and occasionally quoted an old phrase by Isaac Newton that said, "What goes up must come down."

Looking back, I think the scripture from Proverbs 16:18, "Pride goes before destruction, and a haughty spirit before a fall," was more applicable to my situation.

Transitions

Wow, how life has changed for me over the last few years. I am doing really well, so I must be doing something right, I thought as I traveled up the highway to my routine doctor's appointment. I sat at the jug handle, waiting for the light to change, daydreaming about where I would like to go on my next vacation. As the light changed, I saw the driver beside me admiring the brand new Lincoln I was driving. I was careful not to stare, but it did bring a small smile to my face when I thought about the fact that the car actually belonged to me.

I was halfway across the intersection when I caught a glimpse of the grill of a pickup truck just feet from the front passenger door of my car, and then there was a big boom. I will never forget the sound of the crunching metal and shattering glass. Suddenly, it seemed as if time had slowed down, and I was traveling through a space of complete whiteness. I was unsure what had just happened, but I knew it was not good. For what seemed like an eternity, I felt like I was floating through this big white empty space. I could hear the sound of screeching tires and knew that I was no longer in control of the car or my own body, and then suddenly, there was an eerie silence.

As I lay back in the car seat, trying to get my bearings, I was startled by someone knocking on my car window. "Sir, open the door lock!" Someone yelled as I looked to see where the voice was coming from. Things had stopped moving, but I was still in a fog. It took a few moments for me to process what I was hearing and to try to respond to it. As I looked around, I noticed that I was on the property of a gas station that, only moments ago, I was looking at from across the highway. Then I noticed that all of the windows in my car were shattered except for the driver's window next to my seat. Suddenly, it clicked in my mind that I had been in an accident. The people outside my door were trying to help me. I pushed the door lock button, and the man who was knocking on the glass snatched open the door.

"Don't worry, help is on the way," he said.

"My leg!" I yelled out as the man reached over me to turn off the ignition.

Robert C. Morris

"Just lay still. An ambulance is on the way. You're gonna be okay," he reassured me. The police arrived before the ambulance and gathered my belongings, including my driving credentials. The police asked me several questions while waiting for the ambulance. It seemed like it took them forever to get there. However, it was actually just a few minutes.

A couple of police officers followed the ambulance to the hospital and interviewed me in the Emergency Room. I told them all I could remember was the light changing, crossing the highway, and seeing a truck on my right side. They told me not to worry because the other driver had admitted to being distracted by his girlfriend, causing him to run through the red light and collide with my vehicle. "Your car was destroyed and is being towed away. You're lucky to be alive," said one officer.

After a multitude of tests, the hospital determined that, miraculously, there were no broken bones. They concluded that I had a few contusions and that my leg was probably sprained from hitting the dashboard, so they released me for follow-up care with my medical specialists. At the time, I was so happy to be alive that I had no problem accepting their conclusions despite my high level of pain. While being rolled out of that hospital in a wheelchair, a spirit of humility fell upon me. You talk about being knocked down a notch. This traumatic experience had leveled me to the ground, and my pride had flown out the window. My eyes had been opened to see how the most important thing in life is life. I had experienced how quickly those material things that we think are important can be taken away. I was crying out on the inside. Thank you, God, for sparing my life!

The next couple of weeks were filled with follow-up appointments with several doctors. After ordering MRIs and more detailed tests, the specialists determined that I had a torn ACL in my left knee, a concussion, chest contusions, whiplash, and a severe back sprain that was now causing painful muscle spasms. The treatment began immediately, and I started on a recovery journey of pain and suffering that lasted more than four years.

Transitions

Over the next several years, I would see at least twenty three different specialists and undergo arthroscopic knee surgery, biofeedback therapy, extensive physical therapy, psychiatric counseling, nerve stimulation therapy, tens therapy, intramuscular cortisone injections, chiropractic treatment, massage therapy, and given practically every pain medication that is known to man.

During treatment, I became addicted to a highly addictive painkiller. The strange thing about my addiction is that during the first few years, I did not realize that I was addicted. In my mind, I needed the medication to control the pain, plain and simple. There were moments when I thought about the length of time that I had been taking them, but I needed it to function because the pain was so persistent.

After four years of treatment, the doctors concluded that there was nothing more that could be done to improve my condition. In addition to Darvocet™, I was prescribed a medication called Elavil™ to treat my chronic pain and associated insomnia. The arthroscopic knee surgery had not been successful. Several orthopedic surgeons recommended I undergo a complete knee replacement with artificial ligaments installed. The neck and back spasms continued daily and were usually accompanied by crushing headaches that would almost immobilize me. Through this trying period, I would continue to work. Nothing but faith and tenacity kept me going, and I continued to hope that a better day would one day come.

My orthopedic surgeon sat down with me in his office and compassionately explained what he felt was my prognosis. What I heard was so disheartening that I was numb. He said I probably would not ever be able to walk again without some kind of mobility aid and signed my certificate with the Motor Vehicle Agency for a handicap placard as a permanently disabled person. He also suggested that I consider filing for permanent disability because it is likely that I would soon be completely unable to work. Is he crazy? I am only in my thirties. I can't spend the rest of my life in a wheelchair or a bed waiting for a monthly check, I thought. I knew when I left his office that I had fully rejected his suggestion and plan for the future. Deep inside, I had to keep hope alive and believe a change was on the horizon.

However, no matter how much I rejected the prognosis from the doctor, I also felt such a hopelessness to be able to stop his prediction from becoming a reality. No one really understands what it's like to be in excessive pain daily unless you personally experience it. I would cry almost every day because I felt trapped in a body that brought me what felt like torture. There were so many things that I had just taken for granted about daily life that I was now unable to do. In just a matter of seconds, I had been cast into a new normal. It was like going from my thirties to my nineties overnight. My immobility issues caused me to put on an enormous amount of weight very quickly. The weight gain only complicated my condition. It was seemingly impossible for me to control. The only thing that kept me sane was hope for a better day. It was all I had. I was not about to allow anyone to take that one thing away from me.

As strange as it sounds, the crowds and public speaking, to which I had a serious phobia, were now the very thing that kept me motivated to keep trying to work. I was determined to keep going until I dropped because the alternative to me was a quality of life that I could not accept. If there was ever a time that my faith was tested, it was during this period.

I continued to struggle month after month through what felt like a torment sent from hell. My hope was strong all during therapy and the medical procedures. Because active treatment seemed to strengthen the thought that somehow change would come, and the nightmare would end. However, when the treatments ended, it left me with an end-of-the-road feeling, and my hope for recovery had begun to wane. Still, I refused to give in to what appeared to be the inevitable. But in the back of my mind, I knew I could not continue to struggle too much longer in this condition. Every day seemed like a year. I cried, I prayed, and then I would cry again, trying to make sense of the big "why" question inside of me.

Transitions

One night, as I sat down to eat dinner, I saw a flash of a little boy being molested. Is this another one of those visions like the Atlanta situation? I thought. A few days later, I was sitting at my desk at work, and a similar flash invaded my mind again. Only this time, it was for a longer period with more details. I sat there for a few minutes in a semi-daydream stare. After seeing them a few times, I came to realize that the little boy being molested in those flashes was me. Why am I seeing this? Is there something wrong with me? Where are these thoughts coming from? I tried to ignore them for a while, but the more I wanted to ignore them, the more they seemed to happen. The strange thing is that they would occur without warning or provocation.

Every time I experienced these flashes or visions, I had so many emotions flowing through me that it often put me into what some might call an emotional funk. After seeing these images several times, I came to believe that it could possibly be some flashback from my past, but was it real or just something going wrong with my mind? The more they would happen, the more I would challenge the veracity of it. Real or not, it brought with it a feeling of violation mixed with guilt and shame.

Within a few months, I had reached a point where I had considered getting some counseling with a psychologist who had been highly recommended by a friend. I still was not sure that this was the way to go. I needed some confirmation on the idea.

Sitting at dinner one night with my mother, I just blurted it out. "Mom, I'm having a problem!"

"What kind of problem, hun?" she responded between slow chewing bites.

"Well, I keep having what I think are flashbacks of something I believe happened to me as a child. They just come up at any time and any place. I almost feel like I'm losing my mind," I said.

"You mean about what happened with Steven when you were six years old?" she replied. I could feel myself hyperventilating. Tears welled up in my eyes because just those few words confirmed the reality of the images and let me know that what I was dealing with was not my imagination. And as strange as it may seem, just knowing that it was real and not my imagination was therapy within itself. My mind had suppressed those memories for about thirty years in order to deal with the violation and the shame. Obviously, my mind was now trying to deal with it, and the memories had resurfaced from my subconscious.

"I often wondered if you would remember that incident. Now I know that you do," she said. "Do you remember what I did to him? I tried to crucify him and then made him leave the house. Listen, my son, you go to counseling and do whatever you have to do in order to help yourself. People are depending on you to help them, and you cannot help others until you first help yourself," she said encouragingly.

I was relieved to know that this was real and that I was not losing my mind. However, there was a long transitional journey of healing ahead of me. The first step was to find a way to transition from a place of guilt, anger, and resentment to a place of mercy and forgiveness. That journey was extremely difficult because, despite all that I had been taught about Christian principles concerning forgiveness, my emotions overruled my faith. Fortunately, the counseling helped me more than I could have imagined, but the journey was a lengthy emotional roller coaster. The hardest part was finding the strength to forgive without actually confronting my trespasser. I was advised by my counselor that the confrontation would have no benefit to my healing. So, I had to forgive simply out of obedience to God's commands. Once that mission was accomplished, I could feel myself on the road to healing. During this period of emotional healing, I was still living with physical afflictions.

One Sunday, I limped into church on crutches as I had for the last four years. When service was over, an older minister approached me and said, "How long are you going to stay on those crutches?"

"What do you mean?" I replied.

"Well, you teach us about prayer and miracles. Why don't you pray and ask for healing for yourself?"

Transitions

At that moment, I realized that I was always so busy trying to help everyone else that I had not taken the time to sincerely pray and believe God for my own personal healing. It occurred to me that faith taught has to be faith that is practiced. Of course, I would pray daily, but I had not been praying with the same intensity for myself that I had prayed for others. Why shouldn't I expect to receive the same kind of miracle that I had seen others receive?

"You are right, Reverend. Let's pray together," I told him. It was at that very hour that I received one of the greatest miracles in my life. After we prayed, I put down my crutches and cautiously took a few steps and then a few more. Frightened that I would fall, I would only take a few steps at a time and then sit down. The rest of the day, I continued to get up and take a few steps to see if I could still walk without a crutch or cane. I did this over and over again throughout the next few days until my confidence grew and the fear of falling subsided.

Something supernatural had taken place, and it was hard to accept because I had been in a disabled position for so long. My condition had produced in me what I call a mindset of complacent acceptance. Although there is a difference between complacency and acceptance, in my case, I felt like they worked together. Because I had come to accept my condition without any longer questioning it. However, the miracle happened so quickly that it didn't take long for me to accept the change.

On my next visit to the doctor, he ordered another MRI scan and compared it to the scan images four years prior. The torn and considered irreparable ligaments in the previous scans were now repaired and intact. Even the scars that were on my knee from the arthroscopic surgery were no longer visible.

"Well, I'll be damned, I cannot explain this one," said the surgeon. He may not have known what happened, but I fully understood what had occurred. The impossible had become possible, and I had learned another valuable life lesson. Never accept your current situation as the final verdict because with each new day comes the possibility of change.

Once again, I was transitioning in my faith and being equipped to meet the challenges of the days ahead.

Being delivered from my physical affliction, I began to focus more on the need for companionship. I was almost forty years old and still single. My bachelor status left me open to much scrutiny and discussion as to why I was still unmarried. I had many, and I do mean many, dates, affairs, and short-term courtships, most of which I kept away from the church for obvious reasons. In my opinion, some church people thrive on gossip, and some can be downright vicious.

A perfect example was a couple of years after starting my pastorate; I brought a young lady that I was dating to church with me. Some of the congregants questioned her in an interrogating manner. Others whispered about her and stared at her so intensely that she told me she never wanted to step foot inside my church again. I learned pretty quickly how relationships could be ruined by the intrusive and busybody nature of some church people. I did not desire to live a life of dating without a permanent companion. Still, I also had a lot of baggage, making it very difficult for anyone to get close to me. I eventually gained the nickname of Love 'em and Leave 'em Bob. It was not something I was proud of, but it was how I was emotionally structured.

One day, as I was finishing up church service, I looked into the choir, and one particular choir member caught my attention. Evelyn was quite beautiful. I could tell from just a glance that she was a classy young lady. I remembered that I was told by the presbytery when they installed me as pastor, "Whatever you do, never date anyone in this church!" It was explained to me that the church had been through a series of tumultuous meetings resulting from accusations of former pastors dating within that congregation. It is also true that pastors dating within their own congregations usually end up in a problematic situation.

Despite the warning, I could not ignore the attraction. I tried not to be obvious, but sometimes Evelyn would catch me staring, and she would just smile back at me. One day, I got up enough nerve to ask her

Transitions

out to dinner. Surprisingly, she said yes. Wow, I thought, dreams really do come true.

Evelyn and I became friends first, which I believe is very important for a successful relationship. We enjoyed many of the same things and spent a lot of time traveling, eating dinner, and watching movies. It seemed we could not stay away from each other for any length of time. Evelyn seemed to love me for me, which is no easy feat. She often spoke about how she would never interfere with my ministry and understood the sacrifices of the profession. When the subject would come up about possibly being a pastor's wife, she recognized that it would be challenging but felt that she was up to the task and would try to be supportive.

This relationship seemed too good to be true. Evelyn met every expectation of what I thought would be the perfect companion. It also helped that my family adored her; she seemed to blend in with everyone. After a year, I decided that I would pop the question and ask her to marry me. I planned to do it while we were celebrating her birthday at dinner. I spent weeks trying to perfect the plans that were in my head. I am sure the salespeople at the jewelry store got tired of dealing with me. I kept them busy for the greater part of the entire day, trying to decide on the right engagement ring for the proposal. I wanted that evening to be really special, so I made a reservation at a fancy restaurant in a quaint little town about 20 miles away from my house. I pretended to go to the restroom and had a talk with the manager. I explained my plans and asked if they would help me to surprise her.

After dinner, we would order dessert, and instead of the dessert, the waiter would bring out a covered dish with the ring box under it. Evelyn was a little hesitant about having dessert, but I talked her into it, and everything worked out perfectly. It was a night that I will never forget. The weeks that followed came with a lot of pressure from family and friends to set a wedding date. Everyone had a suggestion, but I felt that she and I needed to sit down and decide most of the details for ourselves.

Unfortunately, my life could not have been any busier, leaving very little time for us to discuss our wedding plans. I was recently promoted on my job, requiring me to take courses at a regional university. At the same time, I was studying toward my doctorate degree in divinity. The workload and pressure made it very difficult to handle my responsibilities at the church. There were times that I could not even remember how I got home at night because of exhaustion. I was constantly apologizing to Evelyn for being so busy. Despite feeling ignored, Evelyn would tell me that she understood my busy schedule and encouraged me to keep on track whenever I wanted to give up, "All of your efforts will pay off in the long run.

However, I'm not sure whether it was her need for more attention from me or just the real her coming to the surface, but not long after our engagement, her attitude toward my busyness and career decisions seemed to change. It started with small questions about my career path and critiquing the decisions that I would make. It was not always straightforward, but most of the time, there were subtle little hints that she did not agree with or approve of certain things. When I would question her about it, she would simply say, "Well, never mind, it's just not the way that I would do it."

I could have accepted advice or constructive criticism, but her persistent critiquing was beginning to feel more like a control issue. Evelyn's critiquing became a very big contention point for us. One of the things that most people do not understand about me is how I can appear so outwardly passive and yet be such a determined, strong-willed person on the inside. If I believe that I have been divinely set on a certain path, then nothing, and I mean nothing, can change my mind about it. I also had what I called a split personality when it came to my handling of secular work as opposed to the way I conducted myself at the church.

Many times, because I was in charge at work, some challenges required me to be aggressive, demanding, and even brash in order to get things done. Yet, when I was at the church, I tried to display an attitude of politeness and reasoning to get things done. The real me was somewhere in the middle of the two.

Transitions

As the days went by, Evelyn and I seemed to disagree more and more on many issues. Trying not to be offensive sometimes made me feel as if I was walking on eggshells. One of the biggest obstacles for me was after living single for almost forty years, it was very difficult for me to change or to conform to what someone else thought that I should be. Our moments of disagreement bothered me greatly. However, being naive to serious relationships, I just assumed that this was what most couples went through when trying to blend their lives together. Sort of what I would call merging pains. So, I continued on, determined to give the relationship my best effort.

Evelyn was more open to discussing personal issues with others than me. She would often discuss some of the things that she felt strongly about in our relationship with members of her family as well as mine; I imagine this was sometimes to vent and others to get support for her point of view. However, since I had led such a private and reclusive lifestyle, having others knowing about my private conversations became extremely infuriating to me. Especially when they would come to me offering unsolicited advice on a particular issue or matter.

We struggled for some time, trying to work through a lot of issues. I believe that many of our disagreements were caused by two very strong yet different personalities trying to come together. I had finally learned how to love freely, and yet irreconcilable differences was another blockage in the path to accomplishing that goal. After several more intense disagreements, we decided to call it off. The breakup bothered me much more than I chose to let her or anyone else see.

I cannot explain in words the feelings of failure I struggled with for a long time after that. What is wrong with me? I asked myself over and over again. Am I completely incapable of having a harmonious and satisfying relationship? Am I so damaged by my past that it has totally destroyed my future? Am I so stuck in my ways that I cannot compromise and accept the weaknesses and strengths of another person? Why can't I just love unconditionally and not sweat the small stuff?

I hated myself for the poor relationship skills that were entrenched inside of me. As a result, I retreated again into a shell and a place of non-committed dates and flings that brought only temporal satisfaction with no feeling of belonging or hope of any kind of commitment.

The strange thing is that after the breakup, I never sought companionship. Still, I discovered that I never had to be alone unless I wanted to. There was always someone interested in keeping me company. I think it might have been because I was somewhat successful and held two prominent positions. And then I had heard it said by many that I was "kinda easy on the eyes". Whatever the reason, I was not happy, and I began to pray for a change. I knew the road I was on was not the one I wanted to continue traveling. At some point, there must be a transition of my mindset and desires that would change my relationship skills for the better.

And be not conformed to this world: but be ye transformed by the renewing of your mind, that ye may prove what is that good, and acceptable, and perfect, will of God. Romans 12:2

Chapter Eight

A WAY OUT OF NO WAY

Our church was worshiping in a building that was once a bowling alley that was later converted to a movie theater and then renovated to serve as a storefront church. The building was over 100 years old and needed repairs, so it was crumbling right before our eyes. We had limited heat in the winter from an antiquated boiler that broke down almost every week. There was no air conditioning in the summer. A few ceiling fans hung about twenty feet above us, and some did not work. There were no windows to open, so on extremely warm days, we would open all the emergency exit doors, hoping that an occasional breeze from outside would pass through.

The ground floor was built on a declining slant that descended approximately four feet below street level. Many times, when there was a major rainstorm, the street drains would back up, and the sanctuary would flood with water. The male church officers and I would roll up our pant legs and wade through, sometimes up to two feet of water.

There were rumors that the City Council of our town was working on a proposal that would allocate money for an Urban Renewal Project. The project would affect a three-block area that included our church building. The initial plan was to acquire some properties and renovate others, including the church, while bringing some tax ratables into the area. That plan was scrapped, and a decision was made to declare the neighborhood blighted and raze the entire area, including the church. We were never notified about the change of plans. We would have missed the public hearing except for the concern of one city official who made us aware of what seemed like an unstoppable plan. We learned of the plans just a few days before the public hearing and City Council vote. It appeared that what we had before us was an impossible situation to change.

There is an old saying that you cannot fight city hall, but I sure as hell was going to try. The tenacious part of my character was going to see to that. The plan meant we would have to find somewhere else to worship or simply dissolve our fellowship. We had no money and could barely keep the lights on, and only a handful of members were on the church roll. There was very little value to the old, dilapidated building where we worshipped. A check for that would probably be just enough to buy us a tent. As hopeless as it seemed, I was still determined to find a path for us because giving up was not an option.

It appeared that the iron-fisted mayor of our city was gung-ho about the redevelopment plan and had the votes on the council to get it approved. I knew no one at City Hall and had a difficult time trying to schedule a meeting with the mayor. How could we fight when we had no voice? It appeared that we were out there all alone. Yet there was still a small voice speaking to me on the inside, saying, "God will make a way."

I found myself frantic and edgy every day due to the stress and worry over the future of our church. It was especially difficult because I am so used to being proactive, but in this situation, I was forced to be reactive, not knowing what was coming our way next. However, the greatest lesson I learned from the whole experience was that when you say that you have faith and depend on God, you have to learn to be patient and wait on him. I had always been a take-charge-right-now person with very little patience for waiting. If it can be done, then let's do it now was my motto, but in this situation, I had no choice but to be patient.

Transitions

The pressure was enormous, with constant questions coming from the congregants, family members, and friends. There were constant rumors all over the place, and most of them presented a negative outcome for us. I wanted to be encouraging and reassure those around me with comforting answers. Still, it just seemed like there were no positive answers to be found.

It was only a couple of days in advance that we received an official notice from City Hall about a public hearing regarding the finalization of their urban renewal plans. Our attendance at that meeting seemed fruitless because it was obvious that the mayor supported the proposed plan. The mayor did not work alongside the city council, but he controlled the city council and always got what he wanted. He was a dictatorial leader who received very little pushback from other city officials. It appeared that he and the council had previously discussed this matter. It was evident at the meeting that their minds were already made up no matter what was discussed in the public forum. The decision would be to adopt the proposal, and our church would have to sell the property and move.

"It's a little early to talk money, but your building is almost worthless. However, you will probably get a little something for the land if you need money to help you move," the mayor remarked. "It's not going to be much, and if you want my recommendation, I would probably split the money among the members, and everyone can go to another church. God knows there is an abundance of churches in the area," the mayor concluded.

Was he right? Was this the end of a ministry that had occupied that corner of the city for almost 40 years? But again, I heard that voice speaking to me, saying, "Just wait and say nothing," and that is precisely what I did.

One afternoon, I was in class at a State University taking a course on Environmental Science for my job. I was seated next to a friendly young lawyer. "Hi, my name is Donald Jackson," he said as we shook hands and began to share war stories about our careers. He was new to a prestigious law firm about 10 miles north of the church and excited about his future. I explained to him that I was happy about my career, but my first love was the church. I briefly shared with him the struggle we were involved in with our city and how stressful it had been dealing with that situation.

After class, Donald asked, "Do you like Portuguese food?" "There's a great Portuguese restaurant not far from my office where we can have dinner and further discuss your dilemma," he added.

I was somewhat weary of going anywhere with a stranger, but my senses told me that it was okay as long as I met him there and drove my own car, so I agreed to dinner. "Great, meet me at my office, because I have to stop there after class to finish up a few things and then we can go to the restaurant from there. Here's my office address," Donald said. I did not want to tell him how directionally challenged I was, so I requested that he jot down specific directions just to ensure that I would not get lost as I usually did when traveling.

Donald told me that if I could just make it to the main boulevard, I could not miss the office complex because it was the largest building in the area. However, I did not expect to see what I saw, which was a beautiful and enormous complex that must have held at least a thousand offices. As I took the elevator to his floor, I thought how unreal it felt to be in this building as a guest and not for some kind of litigation.

"Hi, I'm here to see Mr. Jackson," I told the receptionist.

"Oh yes, he's expecting you. Let me take you to the waiting lounge. Help yourself to some snacks and beverages, and he'll be with you shortly," she said kindly.

Wow, what a place! This is like something right out of a movie. I thought to myself. Not wanting to ruin my appetite, I grabbed a bottled water from the self-service bar. I had just opened it and taken a sip when Donald walked into the room. "How about if we walk instead of driving? It's just a couple of blocks away," Donald said. You could tell that he was really into keeping fit and it was a warm and clear evening so I agreed. The restaurant was small, but the decor was outstanding. Donald seemed excited about being there and could not wait to recommend a few dishes he had previously tried and found to be superb. "So, tell me, why are you at this church so far away from home? Is this like a calling?"

"Well, yes," I replied. "I just believe this is where I'm supposed to be, and I feel like I'm on a mission. But now we are being pushed out by the city, and it looks like we have no recourse to their actions," I said sadly.

"Maybe, maybe not. The way I see it is that your biggest problem is that you don't have a voice, but if you can publicly draw attention to the unfairness of your circumstances, just maybe the city will hear and at least work with you. After all, the last thing any politician wants is bad publicity," said Donald. "I have a friend who is a reporter at the largest newspaper company in town that might be able to help you. Here, give John a call and tell him I referred you." He handed me a number scribbled on a business card. "Now, let's feast on this meal tonight. We can worry about our problems tomorrow," Donald said as he dug into his food.

I contacted John the very next day. He was very interested in writing an article to tell our story. He agreed with Donald that the best course of action against City Hall would be to fight their decision in the court of public opinion. However, when John arrived at the church to do the interview, I chose not to be there. Instead, I asked our Associate Minister to meet with him. Once again, my shy nature had kicked in. I wanted to avoid being photographed and in the limelight. Also, the Associate Minister and his family had been a part of that church for more than 20 years. They knew far more about its history and the community than I did. I also thought it would be wise to let someone else play the bad cop if the city leaders decided they wanted to meet with me. This would ensure that any possible meeting would not be tainted by anything I might have said to the newspaper. The Associate Minister did an excellent job representing us in the interview, and the article made the front page.

Robert C. Morris

A few days after the newspaper article had run, the phone constantly rang with people calling to express their opinions and support. "Did you see the paper? We made the front page and a full inside page with photos," said one caller who was also a congregant at the church. Wow, this is really good news, I thought, but the news pulled me into a transitional period by opening a door that forced me out of my comfort zone. I was propelled into the forefront of a lengthy battle and negotiations that no one could have ever prepared me for. All the odds seemingly against us made me wonder if I was crazy to take on this challenge.

My schedule often prevented me from eating a balanced meal, so I would usually fill up on fast foods and eat it between church meetings at my desk. I was just finishing a burger and cola when there was a knock at my office door. "Come in," I shouted loudly. One of the deacons walked in, followed by a Bishop from a neighborhood church. "Oh wow, you're Bishop Edmonds!" I blurted out, somewhat starstruck and lost for words. Bishop Edmonds was well-known throughout the region as a great preacher and a well-connected person on the political front. We had never personally met but had only seen each other in passing. I could not believe that someone of his prominence was actually standing in my crumbling little office.

"Well, aren't you gonna ask me to have a seat? He said in a curious voice.

"Oh, I'm sorry, Bishop, please sit down." It's such a pleasure to meet you," I replied humbly.

"It's good to meet you too. I've heard a lot about you. Then I saw the article in the paper and decided it was time for us to meet. I want you to take Friday off so that we can talk and then go out for a bite to eat," he added.

"Um, okay, sure," I replied, all the while thinking how he did not ask but simply told me what to do. Nevertheless, everything within me knew better than to reject an invitation from such an influential person. Of course, I took the following Friday off, and we met to eat lunch at a small

Transitions

diner not far from the church. Bishop asked me many questions about my experience and my career. He said, "You know, I oversee many churches from the East Coast to the West. Some of which would be very happy to have you as their pastor. As a matter of fact, I have a church in Washington, D.C. that would just love you. It's a large membership, and they would take good care of you."

"How would that work with my job here?" I said.

"You go there on the weekend and come back here to work on Monday. They have a parsonage that you can stay in on the weekend. Besides, after you get your feet wet there, you will probably want to quit your job and stay there full-time. I was working as a civil engineer when I started my church, but I have never been so happy or prosperous until after I quit my job and focused solely on serving the church," Bishop proudly said.

"Well, right now, I am committed to this building project. Once it is completed, I will think long and hard about your offer."

"Come on, let's go." Bishop motioned for me to pick up the check and leave a tip.

"Have you ever ridden in a Mercedes?' asked Bishop Edmonds.

"No sir," I replied.

"Leave your car and we'll take my Mercedes. I have some people that I want you to meet," he said.

Bishop was on the Board of Directors at a well-known bank and took me to their regional headquarters to meet some other board members to discuss financing options for our new church building project. "You do realize that you will have to build a new church? He said.

"Build? How? I was hoping we could renovate to match the redevelopment facade. We don't have any money. Our building is worth next to nothing. We have no assets or credit. Who would even consider lending us any money?" I asked doubtfully.

"Where is your faith?" Bishop replied. "Just do your homework and start preparing for the task. With prayer, it will get done," he added.

Robert C. Morris

When we arrived back in town, I had a lot of information with plenty of homework and more questions than I could contain in my memory. My analytical side needed answers. I decided the best way to handle the abundance of questions was to start a daily journal and write down every question and answer in my notebook. Every day, I found my mind searching for answers to my "what if" questions and the homework assignment I had been given. Each day's work was as if I was laying a single brick to the foundation of a skyscraper. It seemed like such an impossible task was placed inside of such incapable hands, but I continued to hope and pray as I continued to lay one single brick after another.

I was overwhelmed by the enormity of the assignment, and almost every day, I wanted to give up. I had heard it said that pastors who take on the project of building a church either die from the stress or finish the project extremely ill. After examining the history of those that I knew who took on such an assignment, I found that saying to be very accurate. So then, why am I doing this? I would ask myself. I would try to encourage myself, but then I would look at our lack of vital necessities, sometimes hindering my faith. We had no money, and our property was almost worthless. We had just a few dozen faithful members in our fellowship. We had no voice with the city administration. I had no knowledge or experience with construction. Our church lacked organizational structure. No matter how great our ideas or hopes may have been, the situation seemed just plain hopeless. However, I once heard someone say, "The best way to fail is to give up," so I was determined to continue to try even if I failed.

As the days went on, something strange began to happen. One by one, people who could have some effectual impact on changing our situation were just literally walking into my life. This was not by chance or accident. I did not seek these people out, but I believe a divine hand was bringing us together to fulfill a greater purpose than all of us.

I must admit that I was still filled with doubt. However, so many puzzling things started happening. Slowly, I began to see that this was

Transitions

not my battle and that someone greater than me was orchestrating things. First, a millionaire banker/pastor walks into my office and befriends me. Then, a Methodist Pastor in the next town called me to offer his services and advice. After that, a group of community ministers offered their support by speaking to a group of local politicians. Then, I had the idea to reach out to churches in neighboring communities and their regional association of churches with petitions soliciting their support. If I could show city officials that we were not all alone in this struggle, we might get them to listen. The response from the churches was absolutely overwhelming. With the help of our church association moderator, we received responses from not only local churches but also signatures representing approximately 40,000 people across several counties in our state. I was a little hopeful that with their backing, we might just gain some kind of leverage to negotiate.

I decided we would deliver the petition of 40,000 signatures to the mayor and city council by hand while they were in public session. I thought the effects of that move would have a greater impact than sending them by mail. After all, the last thing any politician wants is negative publicity, and we wanted to make it clear that publicity was precisely what we were ready to give them, whether negative or not.

Afterward, we received several calls from city hall inviting us to meetings to try to devise an amicable solution, but those meetings proved to be fruitless. Our request was pretty simple. If you want us to move, help us accomplish that goal. However, the city would not commit to any kind of financial assistance. Still, the fact that they would not vote to finalize their plans and dismiss us said that we had their attention.

The uncertainty surrounding the situation kept us praying. We had so many meetings to discuss our hopes and plans that we practically lived at the church. There were few members, but almost everyone seemed committed to the cause. A motion was placed before the city council to bring their plans to a final vote. Not only did our congregants show up, but the chambers overflowed with supporters from churches throughout the region. While they voted to move forward with the project, the mayor asked that the motion be amended to add helping the church to relocate. That motion was approved. We spent the next few months negotiating with the City over amicable solutions. The final agreement was that the city would purchase our old building at our asking price and donate the land on the corner adjacent to our building where some abandoned homes were sitting. Even with the proceeds and the land, there would still not be enough revenue to build a new church, so we had to consider applying for a mortgage. This was not a complete victory, but it gave us hope that a way was being made out of no way.

Fear ye not, stand still, and see the salvation of the Lord... Exodus 14:13

Chapter Nine

FATAL ATTRACTION

The church building project was underway. I did not know then that it would take seven years from planning to completion. The meetings and decisions that needed to be made daily seemed endless. Although I lived and worked more than sixty miles from the church, I was there for every meeting with the architect, bank officials, contractors, board members, and church membership. It was extremely stressful to work all day and then travel afterward for meetings that sometimes went on past midnight in a building with no heat or air conditioning. I knew deep down that I was pushing my faculties to the limits. I felt almost every day that I could not go any further, but my tenacious nature, combined with my faith, would not allow me to give up.

Many friends warned me of the danger zone in which I was traveling and encouraged me to pace myself and take breaks. So, I started taking short trips when I could squeeze in a day or two. Unfortunately, many of those trips turned into workcations. No matter how hard I tried to decompress, I was still unable to relax. I received an invitation to come to Arkansas to run a three night revival service. I immediately blocked those dates on my calendar. I said to myself, "This is what I need. I need more preaching experience. This will also give me a much-needed getaway.

However, as soon as I committed myself to the assignment, every problem that could get in the way seemed to arise. This is truly a perfect example of Murphy's Law, I thought, but I decided to resolve whatever issues I could and leave the rest until I returned from Arkansas.

Being my worst critic, I became very disappointed with my revival service performance. I found myself questioning whether being a revivalist was something I should be trying to do. Besides, I had none of the gifts that most great revivalists possess. My gifting areas were prayer and teaching, and my teaching skill was more on a Sunday School level.

So, at the end of every revival service, I would have a brief prayer service, and many times, miracles were performed right in the service. This kept the people coming back night after night. They wanted to see what miraculous thing would possibly happen the next night. Little did I know that this was a training course for me. I was being transitioned into a prayer warrior who God would not only wrought miracles through, but it allowed me to be instrumental in his performance of miracles and reveal spiritual mysteries to me that would make me victorious in the challenges that lay ahead.

"Ahh," I said as I stretched out on the hotel bed. I should sleep well tonight, I thought. Being that it was the last night of the revival services. I was exhausted and had just drifted off to sleep when the telephone rang. I wondered who it could be calling, seeing that it was almost midnight? All kinds of things were going through my mind as I groped the nightstand in the dark, searching for the telephone. "Hello," I said with a soft, groggy voice.

"Hello, Pastor, this is Evangelist Sarah, the woman you prayed for tonight," the voice on the other end said.

"Oh, hi, yes, I remember you. Is there something wrong?" I replied.

"No, I just wanted to thank you for helping me get clarity on something tonight," Sarah said excitedly. "You see, I am engaged to be married, and God showed me tonight that the man I am engaged to is

Transitions

not supposed to be my husband. I had a dream a few nights ago, and you were in it. And when I saw you tonight, I realized that God sent you here to Arkansas to help change my life. I could really use some counseling on how to deal with my situation," she said.

You belong to a church and have a Pastor, correct? I asked.

"Yes," she responded in a reluctant tone.

"Well then, your pastor is the one that should be counseling you," I said.

"Ooh, ummm, I guess I could talk to him, but it won't be easy. You see, the problem is that I am engaged to him, and in my dream, we were walking down the aisle to exchange vows, but when I looked at him, it was not him; it was a man who looked like you. What do you think that mean?" she said.

"I really don't know," I responded.

"Well, I will speak with him and call you and let you know what he says," she said in a dejected tone.

"Okay, well, good luck and have a good night," I said as I hung up the phone. Oh crap, she has my business card with my church and home telephone numbers on it. So, I will probably hear from her again, I thought as I drifted back off to sleep.

Making my way home the next morning was quite a venture. Finding my way through the back woods of Arkansas to the airport was a real challenge with my poor sense of direction. The host pastor had given me detailed directions, which I had carefully written on paper. However, there is something about highway travel and me that just does not mix.

I arrived at the airport just a few minutes before takeoff and landed in Philadelphia on a smooth sailing flight. As much as I had enjoyed getting away, I could fully appreciate the saying, "There is no place like home." It was back to the same daily routine, the same problems, same faces, but still, there was nowhere like home.

About a month later, on a Wednesday evening, I arrived home from prayer and Bible study around 10:00 p.m. I took a moment to call my buddy Harold from work to shoot the breeze and talk about some of the events of that day. I had been in the house only about 10 minutes when the doorbell rang. "Is that someone on your door this time of night? Harold asked.

"Yes, it must be some kid playing a prank or something. Hold on a moment while I peep through the blinds to see who is out there," I said.

"Oh my gosh, Harold, you will never believe this," I yelled into the phone receiver. "'Do you remember the woman I told you about from Arkansas?? She is on my door!" I said excitedly.

"What? On your door? Get the hell out of here!" said Harold. "What are you going to do? You don't need to go to that door because that b**tch sounds like she's crazy.

"No, I will just ignore her and call my cousins in Arkansas tomorrow to see if they know what is going on," I said. The doorbell stopped ringing after about ten minutes, but about an hour later, the phone started ringing incessantly. There were numerous calls that night that the caller ID said were from the Howard Johnson Hotel in Philadelphia, but I refused to answer and just let the answering machine pick them up.

Judging from the frequency of the calls, I concluded that Evangelist Sarah was staying at the Howard Johnson Hotel. She continued to call about every ten minutes for hours, never leaving a message. Eventually, I unplugged the phone from the wall in an effort to get some sleep. I lay awake for hours trying to make sense of the situation and eventually drifted off to sleep.

I got up around 5:30 a.m. the next morning, thinking I would get an early start for work in case Sarah decided to return. Figuring that Philadelphia is about thirty miles away, it would take her at least an hour in rush hour traffic to get back to my house. I planned to be out of the house before 7:00 a.m. and make some calls from work to find out what this was all about. Just as I was grabbing my car keys, the doorbell rang. No, no, no! I said to myself as I peeped through the blinds. It was her again, standing on the front porch of my townhome. There were about four hundred homes in the community, and they all looked exactly alike. It was a new development, and the street names had not yet been

Transitions

assigned. I was on the backside of a cluster facing the woods with no number on my door.

How did this woman from out of state find my place when I never gave her my address? A sense of panic started to set in, and my imagination was running wild. Although I did not fully understand what was happening, I knew it was not good, and it was time to get some outside help.

I picked up the phone, called my cousins in Arkansas, and woke them out of their sleep. "Debbie, do you remember that woman Evangelist Sarah from the revival? She is at my door! I yelled.

"On Your door?" Cousin Debbie said with shock in her voice.

"Yes. She was here last night. She kept calling here from the Howard Johnson in Philadelphia, and now she's back again. Why is she here? How did she even know where I lived?" I said with a panicked voice.

"Oh My Gosh, I am so sorry. This is all my fault," said Debbie. "She said she wanted to write you a letter, and I gave her your address. Give me the number to the Howard Johnson. I will try to call her and see what is going on in her head."

Evangelist Sarah knocked and rang the doorbell incessantly for the next hour. I decided not to go to the door. Not knowing her state of mind, she could start a conflict that might get me into trouble. She could perhaps rip her dress and say that I attacked her. Who knows what was going on in her head, and I was not about to find out.

My Sister and I had always been close, so I decided to call and tell her about the situation. "I'll be right over," she said.

My Sister lived about fifteen minutes away and arrived shortly after our conversation. She said she didn't see anyone in the parking lot or near the house when she walked in. However, just a few minutes later, the doorbell rang. "She must have been sitting in the next parking lot watching the house. Let me handle this," my Sister said.

I could hear a voice from the front door asking if I was at home.

"No! Who are you?" My Sister asked.

Robert C. Morris

"Ummm, my name is Sarah. I met him in Arkansas last month. He mentioned that he had high blood pressure. I brought him some pills. Would you please see that he gets these? They really will help him a lot,"

"Yeah, okay, bye," my Sister said as she opened the screen door, retrieved the package and closed the door quickly. "I can't be angry with her. You can tell she's a disturbed soul, shaking like a leaf," my Sister commented.

A few minutes later, I left for work. I called my cousin Debbie around noon to update her on Sarah's latest behavior and received more concerning information. "I have some bad news," said Debbie. "My daughter works at the bank, and she said Sarah came in last week and withdrew all her money. She told my daughter that God had sent her a husband, and she was getting married and moving out of state. I did manage to reach her at the Howard Johnson Hotel. She was very angry. She said you acted like a punk and sent your girlfriend to the door instead of coming out to talk to her. She said that she is not leaving until you talk to her. If you don't talk to her now, she will be at your church on Sunday, and you'll have to face her then. There is something really wrong with her!"

An eerie feeling came over me. I was beginning to believe this was not just a case of someone with a mental disorder; it smelled with an aroma of demonic influence. I could sense the demonic presence just from all of my previous experiences in life with evil forces.

There was no doubt in my mind that this woman was being influenced by Satan to distract and torment me. It was weird, bizarre. I had difficulty explaining the situation to others because most people believed I must have done something to cause it. I could sense that my help from people would be limited and that it was definitely praying time.

Although I had only been involved with the exorcism of demons in a direct confrontation, I wondered if I could exercise that same authority over a demonic spirit even from a distance. I began to pray fervently almost every hour over this situation.

Transitions

Each day, I looked over my shoulder and sneaked in and out of my house, wondering if she was watching from across the street or hiding in the bushes just outside my door. Every day I arrived home, a handwritten letter from Sarah was slipped under my door. One letter was eight pages long. She rambled on and on, quoting Bible verses and speaking about her dreams and visions. I talked to the local police, and they basically said they could not help me unless she actually committed a crime. Just leaving me a few letters was not a crime. I asked my cousins in Arkansas to call Sarah at the hotel again and let her know I had contacted the police. If she came back to my house, they would arrest her. Of course, this was not true, but I hoped it would stop her from harassing me. In the meantime, I began fasting and praying fervently against the evil forces confronting me.

I probably didn't get more than three hours of sleep each night leading up to that Sunday. I spent most of my awake hours in prayer, trying to get a clear understanding of what was happening and what I should do next.

Should I forewarn the church members of this impending disturbance? Would telling them about it cause more problems and possibly escalate the situation? Would the church members really believe my story, or would they feel like I might have done something to cause this situation? Even I would have difficulty believing my innocence if it were not happening to me. The predominant thought in my mind was this Sunday is really going to be a mess!

It had to be the power of prayer that changed Sarah's mind. That Sunday morning came, and she never showed up at the church. However, it was an awfully stressful day for me. I was on the edge of my seat every time the church door opened. Her not showing up did not put me at ease. I began thinking that maybe she had gotten lost and would be waiting at my house when I got back home. I drove slowly around my neighborhood, looking carefully for any sign of her, but Sarah was nowhere to be found.

Robert C. Morris

It was as if Sarah had just disappeared into thin air. No more letters. No more calls. No more ringing my doorbell. She was just gone. I called my cousin in Arkansas to see if she had heard from Sarah. She told me that Sarah had indeed arrived back in Arkansas. Of course, my mind would not accept that this mysterious stalker who had struck a note of fear in me that I had never experienced before was gone for good. For months, I drove around my neighborhood when returning home, thinking that she might have returned. The slightest noise at night would cause me to jump from bed and look around the house as well as out my windows.

This experience changed my life in two major ways. One, I ended up getting a security system. Sadly, to this day, I still do not feel as secure at home as I did before this incident. Number two, I learned that there are times that you must pray about something and then let go and let God, trusting that the end result will be alright. I was expecting to hear or see something that would assure me that my prayers had been heard while facing this dilemma. However, there was no sign, call, or way of knowing that the threat was over. This taught me to pray and trust with blind faith that God will hear and answer prayer and will take even evil things and work them out for your good.

And we know that all things work together for good to them that love God, to them who are the called according to his purpose.
Romans 8:28

Chapter Ten

HEARTBREAK

Several years passed, and the struggle to build a new church building continued. The day had finally come when that project was complete, and we could move into our new house of worship. At this point, we were having worship service in a community center because the structure of the old building was collapsing and had been condemned by the city as unfit for human habitation. Although the community center was convenient, it was not comfortable. Yet, strangely enough, the services seemed much more intimate and uplifting.

Finally, a date was set for our first Sunday Service in the new edifice. We invited everyone from near and far to come and join us in a big celebration. I had been feeling very tired and knew that I desperately needed some rest. However, there was just too much to be done. I figured that I would be able to take a break after the move-in celebration. I would come home from work some days so exhausted that I had to crawl on my hands and knees just to get upstairs to my bed. It should have been a troubling thing to have to crawl up the stairs, seeing that I was in my late forties, but somehow I had gotten used to doing so on occasions when I was drained.

Although I had been exhausted before, this particular night felt different from all the other times. I had developed a fever. I was nauseous and fatigued to the point that I could barely get out of bed to use the bathroom. I guess I better notify my job that I will be taking tomorrow off, I thought as I placed a message in my assistant's voicemail. Overnight, my symptoms intensified to the point that I found myself in the doctor's office early the next morning. The doctor said, "You, my friend, have the flu." I was ordered to bed with several medications from the pharmacy delivered to my home. This was the only year I neglected to get a flu shot. Now, I had the flu just weeks before our first service in the new edifice.

I had worked and waited seven years for this day. Nothing was going to stop me from being a part of this grand celebration. However, I had so many underlying conditions, such as asthma and COPD, that the virus took a terrible toll on me. I developed many complications. I was confined to bed for thirty one days and stayed sick for almost three months. On the day of the celebration, I pleaded with family members to drive me to the church, which they reluctantly did. I could only sit and watch, but I was just so excited to be there that it really didn't matter to me that I was so sick.

As time went on, I began having more and more difficulty sleeping. Many times, if I did get to sleep, I would be awakened by a nightmare. I would toss and turn most of the night with my mind recalling things over and over again, refusing to shut down. Every time I wake up from a horrible dream, I would drift back off to sleep only to have the same dream all over again. Many nights, I would get up and walk around drinking a bottle of water, hoping that getting out of bed and moving around would break the dreadful dream cycle.

One night, I sat on the side of the bed for a while trying to refocus my mind to think on pleasant thoughts. I hoped that those thoughts would remove the images of the horrible dream I just had from my mind. However, about an hour later, I was again fast asleep, having that same dream all over again. The dream was so vivid and disturbing that I decided to just get up early despite the fact that I would have loved to sleep late on my day off.

Transitions

One particular morning, after having a dream about my mother collapsing from a heart attack, I had a strong urge to call and check on her. I had made it a practice to call and check on her every day because she was living alone and getting up in years. That morning, I called several times, but there was no answer. I found it strange because she hardly ever left the house and almost always answered her phone. Maybe she is in the bathroom or having a really busy morning, I thought. After a couple of hours of calling and leaving messages, I started getting concerned as to why she hadn't called me back. She has caller ID and can see that I called. I tried not to panic, but so many thoughts started rushing through my mind. Those thoughts were exacerbated by the dream that I had just hours before. There is definitely something wrong, I thought as I now began to panic.

As I jumped into my car, I kept talking to myself, trying to stay calm and reminding myself not to speed down the highway. It was about a half-hour drive from my house, and every few minutes, I would push the repeat call on my cell phone, hoping to get an answer. As I pulled up to her townhome, I parked right next to her car. I felt the hood of her car, and it was cold, so I could tell it had not been moved for hours. Walking at a fast pace toward her door, I tried to prepare myself for what I might find. I was praying under my breath, and I could feel myself hyperventilating. I have a key, but I better knock first, I thought. I rang the doorbell, pounded on the door, and then used my key to unlock it.

As I pushed the door open and stepped inside, I noticed a figure walking toward me from the bathroom area. It was her; she was okay. She had a towel wrapped around her head and a big smile on her face. "Oh, hi, hon," she said in a cheerful voice.

"Are you okay?" I blurted out. "I have been trying to reach you on the phone for a while," I said, panicky.

"Oh yes, I heard the phone, but I was washing and dying my hair and could not stop to answer it. Why? Is there something wrong?" she asked.

"Well, no, I just sorta panicked when I couldn't reach you. You see, I had this reoccurring dream last night about you, and it had me kinda upset. Every time I fell asleep, I would have the same dream repeatedly," I said.

"Well now, mister psychic, why don't you sit down and tell me about this dream? She said as we both took a seat opposite each other. After telling her about my dream, she just stared at me in silence for a moment.

Finally, she said, "Well, I guess I better tell you what happened to me the other night. I was awakened out of my sleep with a pain in my chest that seemed to get more painful every few minutes. At first, I thought it was indigestion, but it started affecting other parts of my body. I didn't want to bother anyone in the middle of the night, so I just got up and started walking around praying. After a couple of hours, it eased up, and I was able to sit up in bed and rest. I believe now that it was a problem with my heart, so I called to make an appointment with the cardiologist."

A very strange feeling came over me. It was becoming clear to me that my dream was some kind of warning. I requested that she see her cardiologist right away and assured her that I would go with her to hear the results of any test. Fortunately, we were able to get an appointment with the doctor for the following day.

The cardiologist explained that he believed that she had suffered a heart attack. He chastised her for not calling anyone to assist her because it could have been fatal. He recommended an EKG, Echogram, and catheterization to be done immediately. He said, "You cannot go back home, but you must be admitted to the hospital and tested right now.

The tests revealed exactly what the doctor had suspected; she had indeed had a myocardial infarction. My sister and I were asked to wait in a private conference room to speak with the doctor. The doctor showed us the scans and gave us his diagnosis. The news was not good, and the prognosis was grim. He told us that the tests revealed that because of the heart attack, a portion of the heart muscle was now dead due to a lack of blood flow into the area. The blockage was not due to plaque but to the damage done to the arteries as a result of diabetes and high blood sugar levels. The worst part was that other arteries had also been so severely damaged that they could not be repaired with stints and would eventually

Transitions

fail. "My opinion to you is that you enjoy whatever time you have left together because she cannot make it too much longer with this untreatable condition."

The amazing thing was that when my Mother was told of her diagnosis and prognosis, she did not get upset. She just looked at all of us and simply said, "Well, okay."

I heard the report from the doctor but struggled with denial to accept the reality that my mother would soon no longer be with me. However, in the months that followed her dismal prognosis, I experienced many unusual occurrences that should have served me notice that something major was getting ready to take place.

For example, one day while in church, I glanced over at my mother, who had fallen asleep due to tiredness. However, instead of seeing her hunched over asleep in the pew, I saw her lying flat in a casket. My first reaction was to say, "My mom, my mom." A second later, the minister sitting beside me said, "She's okay; she's just asleep. She's probably real tired."

When I looked back again, all I saw was her sitting up asleep. I could not speak at the moment about what I had seen and should have realized that it was a vision of what was to come, but despite the vision, I was in a deep state of denial.

Months went by without Mother having another single medical emergency. She maintained a normal lifestyle of cooking, shopping, cleaning, attending church, and caring for herself. As a matter of fact, she appeared to be in good physical and mental health for someone eighty years of age. We would attend church together every Sunday, and afterward, we would enjoy a homemade dinner she had prepared at her house. Occasionally, I would take her out to eat at her favorite restaurant.

One Sunday, she told me she had prepared one of my favorite meals, and we could have dinner together at her house. As we pulled up to her townhome, she began to tell me about several small things in her house that needed to be repaired. I was used to having to work for my supper and did not mind because I knew she needed help maintaining her property. We never sat at the dining room table, but we ate from TV trays in front of the TV in the living room.

Just minutes into the meal, there were three sharp knocks on the front door. These raps were so loud that they almost sounded like a hammer banging on the metal frame of the storm door, and it startled me. My first thoughts were, who would bang on the door so hard, and why knock when she has a doorbell? I was less than three feet from the door. I got up to see who was there when my Mother said, "You don't have to get up. That's the bird trying to get inside." I opened the door and saw neither human nor animal anywhere in sight.

About twenty minutes later, the knocking occurred again. I immediately jumped up and snatched open the door. Nothing! There was absolutely nothing within thirty yards of that door. As I stood there bewildered, my mother said, "I told you it's that bird. He's been trying to get in here for a while." She proceeded to tell me that the other day, a big black bird flew in right through her ceiling and went straight down through the floor and into the ground. "You do know what that means, don't you?" she asked.

"Not really," I replied, wondering to myself just what this bird vision could possibly mean. I sensed that it had something to do with an old wives' tale. She was not raised in the South but believed in many of the signs and traditions taught in the Deep South. We continued on with our supper. I later found out that birds in some southern traditions are a sign of death. A bird flying through the ceiling and into the ground was a sign that death was coming to that house.

My mother was very particular about food. Although she would occasionally eat out at a restaurant, she would not eat at anyone else's house, not even her own mother's. It was only late in life that she occasionally ate food prepared by my sister, whom she would refer to as "a great cook." We would always go over to my sister's during the major holidays to enjoy a gourmet meal and some family fellowship. I always

Transitions

asked if I could prepare something to bring to the dinner. I was told to buy dessert, soda, and napkins but never to prepare food.

One particular day, I had fixed a meal that was my best yet. I really wanted someone to try it and give me a pat on the back. So, I convinced my mother to try a little, and amazingly she did. She said it was pretty good, and we agreed that we would prepare a homemade meal together the following Sunday. I immediately ran out and bought an oven stuffer roasting chicken I planned to cook. I couldn't believe it. Was she actually going to eat a meal that I helped prepare? I was so excited. However, it would never come to pass.

Just a few days later, on that Friday morning, I received a call early in the morning from my mother. She was very calm, but I could hear her shortness of breath. She wanted my sister and I to come over immediately because, as she put it, "It's a minor emergency."

I called my sister, and we both headed for Mom's house. We arrived at almost the exact moment. We found her sitting in a recliner in a bathrobe and looking physically well but mentally stressed. "What's going on?" we asked.

"Well, I need you two to clean up this house and then take me to the hospital because it's time," she said.

"Time? time for what?" I asked in a perplexed tone, but I received no reply. I ran and got the blood pressure and blood sugar monitors. Monitoring her stats was something I often did when visiting. The blood sugar was about normal; however, the blood pressure reading was off the charts. Mother said that she hadn't taken her medication for a couple of days. The refill had been ordered and was ready for pick up at the pharmacy. She had asked for it to be delivered, but it hadn't arrived.

I dashed over to the pharmacy to get the medication while placing a call to her primary physician on the way. The blood pressure did not change at all after taking the medication. Finally, I received a call back from her physician. When I explained my findings to him, he told me to get her to the hospital right away because he believed she was having a heart attack. I panicked and resisted taking her at that moment because my dislike for hospitals made me think irrationally. Fortunately, my Aunt came over and transported her to the Emergency Room. The hospital confirmed our worst fears. It was indeed a heart attack. She received treatment just in time to save her life. We were happy to get this news; however, a bigger problem was on the horizon. She was now in kidney failure. They recommended dialysis as a treatment to try to prolong her life.

When approached with the proposal, Mother firmly rejected it. She made it clear that a life of dependence was not for her. My mother felt that dialysis would weaken her to the point that she would become a burden to her children and need constant care. After visiting others, including her mother, in a nursing home, she had gained a morbid fear of them and would rather die than be a patient in one.

I approached her several times about starting dialysis, getting a nurse, and possibly moving in with me. When she mentioned how my house would not support her needs, I would reply, "Then I'll renovate it or move into one that will work for both of us." However, my offer was kindly rejected.

The big surprise was when my brother-in-law suggested she move in with my sister and him. This caught her off guard because it had taken her a while to warm up to him after he married my sister. Mother was not good at hiding her feelings, and her disdain for him early in their marriage was easy to detect. Some years later, they had developed a decent and somewhat cordial relationship.

My brother-in-law's statement shocked my mother so much that she repeated it to me almost every time I visited her in the hospital. It was pretty obvious that she could not understand how he could make such an offer, knowing how she had felt about him in the past. However, despite his shortcomings, he still possessed some of the Southern values that were instilled in him as a child. One was that family ties are important and you should always extend a hand to them in a crisis.

There are many ways to look at the offer to my mother from my brother-in-law. My interpretation is that God used him to help remove a

Transitions

barrier in my mother's heart to prepare her for eternity. Like many others today who profess to be Christians, she still had an area of weakness that needed healing. Whether it was justified or not, her feelings toward him needed to be corrected. And sometimes, all it takes is an act of love and kindness to help heal a relationship that has been broken for years.

A few days later, I walked into my mother's hospital room to find her sitting up in bed, staring at the wall in deep meditation. She was mobile and had no intravenous connections. Many times, when I arrived, she would be sitting in a chair watching TV. She was an avid reader and television watcher, but this time was very different. There was a dead silence in the room. She was sitting in the bed, staring straight ahead, almost as if she was in a trance. I could tell that she was aware of my presence, but she did not look at me. Her eyes were fixed straight ahead, and she did not even blink. I walked over to the bed and said, "How are you doing?"

"The doctors just told me that I am going to die," she replied.

"Who? What?" I questioned.

"Four doctors came in about an hour ago. Two stood on each side of the bed. They said there is no easy way to say this, but you need to prepare yourself because you are gonna die soon." she said in a voice of despair.

I stood there in shock because I could not believe what I heard was true. I could not understand why those doctors would have that kind of conversation with her alone. Why was her family not asked to be present when they told her? Also, why wasn't this discussed with me since I was in charge of her medical decisions? "I will speak with your primary doctor about this," I blurted out, quickly changing the subject.

The primary doctor requested that my sister and I stop by his office so that he could discuss my mother's prognosis with us. He pulled up a chair and gently said, "There's nothing more we can do for your mother. Her kidneys have stopped functioning and her heart is too weak for dialysis. Do you understand what I'm saying? The doctors are right. She cannot survive much longer without functioning kidneys. Do you know what I'm saying?" He said softly to us. Apparently, my sister got the message, but I was in denial. I was still looking at options for my mother's care after she was released from the hospital and rehabilitation center.

The strangest thing about denial is that almost everyone around you can see it, but you are totally unaware of your own state of denial. I had those weird dreams; there were those strange knocks at the door and the prognosis from physicians, but my mind still would not allow me to accept her impending death.

It was the twelfth day since my mother was admitted to the hospital. Her physical appearance and demeanor were about the same. Looking at her from the surface, it was hard to tell she was so ill on the inside. This made it even more difficult for me to break free from my state of denial. However, if anything should have pierced my denial, it should have been my visit on day twelve. "I tried to get out of bed to walk today, and my legs were too weak for me to stand up. You know what that means?" she blurted out shortly after I entered the room.

"Maybe you've been in bed too long and need some strengthening exercises," I replied. I was perplexed by her statements because I was still lost deep in a state of denial.

"I made a deal with God and he is going to take me in my sleep. So, you can take my clothes and shoes home. I won't need them anymore. Did you mail those bills and pay that insurance premium?" she said, seemingly all in one breath.

"Yes, ma'am," I replied as I put her shoes into a shopping bag to take home with me.

"Everything you need is in the safe in my bedroom closet," she said.

I was somewhat curious as to why she was saying these things, but still lost in a state of denial. Perhaps her remarks were a result of a medication, I thought. Her doctor calls me every night when he gets home to review her medications with me and answer any questions I have. I will ask him if there was a change in medication that could have her talking so strangely. However, a review with him that evening

Transitions

revealed that her medications were the same as they had been for several days.

The following morning, I arrived at work at about 8:45 a.m. and was extremely tired. It was as if I had not slept or rested at all the night before. I had been suffering from insomnia for several years, and with the help of a sleeping pill, I managed to get a few hours of sound sleep each night. However, the sleep deprivation combined with stress had taken a great toll on me. My cell phone kept ringing, and the caller ID showed a strange number with no name. Assuming it was a telemarketer or someone calling the wrong number, I did not answer. Besides, I was groggy and irritable that morning and did not feel like talking. A few minutes later, my sister called to let me know that she had just received a call from the hospital, and we needed to get there right away. They had found our mother in her bed, unresponsive and not breathing. My sister and her husband were on the highway heading south because his mother had died three days earlier. They had almost reached the state line when the hospital called about our mother. The hospital had tried to reach me. Unfortunately, that was the call I had refused to answer. "I'm on my way," I said in a panicked tone as I ran out of my work office toward my car.

My sister and I arrived at the hospital around the same time. We walked nervously to the elevator together and took it to the second floor to the Intensive Care Unit. The reception desk nurse informed us that she was in room number two, right across from her desk. As we entered the room, an unforgettable feeling of despair combined with anticipatory grief shook my heart in a way that I would never be able to put into words.

What we saw was a person who had died because their body organs had shut down but had been resuscitated through the use of chemicals and a respirator. But despite their best efforts to keep her blood pressure up, it was constantly falling. She needed additional medication to keep her pulse and her heart beating.

Robert C. Morris

It was apparent from just one look that her body had failed. She was probably poisoned from the lack of organ function because her nervous system had gone haywire, causing involuntary muscle movements in abnormal ways. In my many years of visiting critically ill people, I had never seen anything like it. It was like something from a horror movie. Her body was lying flat and still as if it was completely dead, but her head was oscillating. At the same time, her eyes were wide open and rolling in a fast circular movement, one clockwise and the other counterclockwise. As I stood there in shock and trying to absorb what I was seeing, a nurse came in and said the doctor was on the line and wanted to speak with us.

"I'm sorry, but I do not have good news for you," he said. We found her not breathing and were able to resuscitate her. But her kidneys have not been functional for a while, and her heart is at minimal thrust, so it won't be long before it stops again. Do you wish for us to try to resuscitate her again? Even if we do, it will only stop again,"

At that moment, it hit me. She told me that she was going to pass away in her sleep. Obviously, that is just what happened. Even if they were to resuscitate, assuming they could, what would that do besides prolong the inevitable?

After a brief conversation with my sister, we decided to sign a (DNR) do not resuscitate order. We called family members, and one by one, they rushed to her bedside to join us in saying goodbye. Even my ex-fiancee came to the hospital to offer her support. Her presence at such a difficult time will always be fondly remembered.

We were taught that all of us must die one day and that there is no escaping that transition from this life into eternity. And I must admit that many times, I wondered what it would be like if my mother preceded me in death. But never could I have ever imagined that I would be sitting in a hospital room waiting for her to take her last breath. It was the most agonizing time that I have ever experienced in my life. I cried, and I walked the floor and then cried some more. Doctors came in to examine her frequently, and they just walked away shaking their heads. One

Transitions

Doctor just looked at me, and without saying a word, he walked over and hugged me and then just walked away.

Every minute that passed seemed like an hour, and every hour seemed like a day. It was now 3:00 p.m., and Mother's condition seemed the same. I advised my family that I was going to go and find myself a sandwich and would be right back. I went to the hospital cafeteria, but I did not like their choices. I remembered a deli about a half mile up the road and decided to drive there. My car was parked just 100 feet outside the hospital door. I thought it shouldn't take me more than 15 minutes to run up the street and grab a sandwich.

I had just pulled out of the hospital lot and up to the traffic signal when my cell phone rang. It was my nephew calling to tell me that the doctor was sending someone to remove the respirator tube. "Why? I told them not to remove anything." I shouted.

"No, you don't understand. They have to remove it," he replied.

I said, "You mean?"

"Yes," he said in a sad tone.

"I'll be right there." I frantically hung up the phone, making a U-turn in the middle of the highway. My heart was pounding so hard that I could barely breathe. About a minute later, the cell phone rang again as I pulled into the hospital parking lot. As I answered, I heard my sister's voice on the other end say, "Where are you at?"

"I'm in the parking lot and will be upstairs in a minute," I answered.

"Go home. We can handle everything from here," she instructed me.

"No, I want to come up and…"

"Go home! Don't make me come down to the lobby and embarrass you!" She said in a stern voice as she interrupted me mid-sentence.

"Okay," I conceded.

As much as my instinct was to get back to that room, she and I both knew that it was not something I could handle. In hindsight, I also think that is why I was led to leave the hospital at that particular moment. It was strange that after seven hours of struggling against death, my mother would transition within a few minutes after I left her room. It was as if she was waiting for me to leave.

The ride home was long and difficult. I was filled with a kind of pain that I had never experienced before. It was as if someone had taken a knife and carved my heart right out of my chest. I hyperventilated until I was on the verge of losing consciousness several times. The anguish that I was feeling was new to me. My mind was racing through my fifty years of life, recalling all of the memories from the past. However, none of them brought me any comfort. They just seemed to exacerbate the pain that I was feeling. Where was God? Why did he allow this to happen? He could have at least let me know this was coming! So many thoughts ran through my mind as I began to develop some anger against the God that I had previously come to trust.

Somehow, I managed to get home safely and made it inside. I paced the floor, talking to myself as I wiped my face with paper towels to catch the tears. Suddenly, something inside me broke, and the ability to stand seemed to leave my body. I found myself lying on the kitchen floor in a fetal position and bitterly weeping. There was an overwhelming pain and sadness that paralyzed my entire being. It felt as if someone was sitting on my chest, and trying to take a breath of air was impossible to do. I had never felt anything like it before. I had never felt so helpless and unable to control my emotions. I lay there for hours until I was completely drained and crawled to the bed to lay across it.

Hours later, I gathered the paperwork needed for the funeral service. As I opened my mother's safe, her favorite scent of perfume filled the room. It felt like more than I could handle, but I forced myself to complete the task because Mother had left me executor of her estate and expected me to make sure things got done. I usually leaned on my sister for strength because she is a rock under stress. However, she had again started heading south to attend funeral services for her mother-in- law.

Many times, over the following weeks, I questioned my faith and mental state and wondered if I would ever get free from the pangs of grief. I was familiar with the old saying that "time heals all wounds."

Transitions

However, during the first several years, "time" did nothing to diminish the pain that I was feeling.

Several months passed by, and the intensity of the loss had not diminished one iota. I was prescribed tranquilizers to stabilize my mood. Then, I took an extended vacation, but I found myself still stuck in the first stage of grief. The emotional crash that would bring on extreme sadness and crying was so unpredictable that I never knew when it would surface. So, I had to put what little social life I had on hold to hide it. I had taken a month off from work. Now that I was back, there were many times that I had to hide in the restroom or run to my car to keep others from witnessing those horrible moments of sadness I experienced. I decided that something had to be done because I could not continue to live on this emotional roller coaster. Counseling had worked in the past. Hopefully, it will work for me again this time.

I had a Pastor friend who specialized in psychology. I had confided in him in the past. Perhaps he would be able to help me get a grip on myself. In our first conversation, I walked away very disappointed because his answers seemed so vague, and I felt like he was minimizing my pain. I realize now that, as a friend, it was difficult for him to be very direct with me because he feared that speaking frankly could have impacted our friendship. However, every time we spoke, I noticed that he would say the same thing, "Grief is a process that you cannot control." I heard what he was saying but did not fully understand what he was saying.

One day, as I meditated, his words popped into my mind. Suddenly, it hit me: you always want to be in control of everything, and that is the problem here. In order to transition through the grief process, you must submit to it and work your way through it step by step. It is a process beyond your control. *It is a process, it is a process, it is a process.* I kept repeating to myself. It was about that time that I learned not to fear my daily crying spells but, in a weird way, to embrace them. They were my way of taking baby steps down a long path that would eventually lead me to the next step of the process. Like every other mountain I had climbed or valley I had walked through, I needed to find the faith to give me the strength to believe that there would be a light at the end of the tunnel. However, there was a big hurdle in front of me. I had developed a resentment toward God, and it did not feel like my anger would ever get any better. I still believed that he was there, but I found it hard to speak to him intimately because I was angry that he had allowed this thing to happen.

I spent the next several years in a spiritual and emotional daze. I was functional in my ministerial and occupational duties, but not with the same intensity or drive I had in the past. My heart was broken in such a way like it had never been before, and nothing seemed to ease the pain. Life became a routine roller coaster of emotions. I would go into hilltop mode to get through the day and then fall into the valley once I was alone.

There were times when I actually thought that I was going to have a nervous breakdown. Many people around me, especially some Ministers, said that my change of demeanor was so obvious that they thought my work in ministry would soon be over. Friends would call and say you can call me if you ever think about doing something crazy. It was good to know they cared, but suicide was never considered during my grief. I guess I am just too selfishly in love with life to let go of it.

The thing that bothered me the most about the process was having something controlling my emotions and not having the ability to control it. Forcing upon me unbearable pain that seemed to consume and emotionally paralyze me whenever and wherever it would choose to surface. The grief was consuming me, and it caused me to do some really strange things.

One day, while driving home, I saw an elderly woman out of the corner of my eye sweeping her driveway. "Wow, she looks just like my Mom," I told myself. I immediately swerved the car off the road and into her driveway, coming to a screeching halt. As I jumped out of my car, I

Transitions

could see that the woman was startled by my quick approach, so I spoke to her from a distance, being careful not to run up on her.

"Hi, are you from North Carolina?" were the first words out of my mouth.

"No, why?" she replied.

"Because you look just like my Mom, who is from North Carolina," I said.

"Oh yeah, who is your Mother?" the woman asked.

"Well, she passed away, but you look so much like her. I can bring you a picture and let you see for yourself," I said.

"Oh, okay, well, leave it in the mailbox and put your name and address on the back so I can write and tell you what I think," the woman replied.

As I got back in my car, I realized how insane I must have seemed to that woman. A middle-aged man pulling up at warp speed out of nowhere, talking about how you look like my dead mother. I am sure she asked me to put my name and address on the picture so she could give it to the police. What is happening to me? I thought.

In an effort to get a grip on the grief process, I decided that I might be able to help it along by changing some of my habits and routines. I made a list of things that triggered bad emotional responses in me and decided to remove them from my life. At the very top of the list were the frequent visits to the cemetery. I visited the grave site about five times a year. It brought me no comfort but only pain. Every time I left the cemetery, I was so distraught and drained that I couldn't focus the rest of the day.

Another thing I did was to remove from my presence all of the constant reminders around the house that were in plain view. The third thing I did was seek to repair my relationship with God. I knew he understood my feelings and why I felt it. However, I needed to confirm within myself the specific reasons why I was angry with him and then confess it to him and ask for forgiveness.

Robert C. Morris

In searching my soul, I discovered that I was not only angry because God had allowed my Mother to die but because I believed he gave me no warning that she was about to expire. However, the Holy Spirit revealed to me that God did give me notice that she was getting ready to transition. He reminded me that he had shown me in a dream, he had shown me in a vision in church, my mother told me directly at her home and then again while she was in the hospital. My problem was that every time I was forewarned, I would immediately counter it with denial, which allowed me in my own mind to make the message not real.

I eventually realized that I could not move through the stages of grief because I was stuck between the first two stages, which are denial and anger. This would not allow me to move on to the final stages of grief and develop a new reality and a new normal. Only after I understood these things and prayed constantly for change could I begin transitioning to the next phase of my life. When I accepted these facts, there was finally some relief from the anguish I had been struggling with for years. I could finally begin to move forward with the healing process.

Blessed are they that mourn: for they shall be comforted. Matthew 5:4

Chapter Eleven

DECISIONS

One of the many jobs that I have taken early in my career was to work as a management trainee in a local bank. It was a requirement that all banking employees take teller training courses before functioning in any capacity in the bank. The training classes were held in a building at a remote location that was set up to resemble an actual bank with a vault and various teller stations. We would spend a great deal of time role-playing there as if it were a functioning local bank branch. Occasionally, a bank executive or some management personnel would come by to speak with us and share some of their varied experiences in the banking industry.

Near the completion of the training courses, one of the regional vice presidents came by to congratulate and motivate us. He was a guy who was well up in years and walked slowly but with great confidence. At the end of his speech, he decided to have a brief question-and-answer session. Although it was decades ago, I still remember one question and answer that stood out in my mind then and still guides my thinking today. The man was asked by a very ambitious young man if he could give him some advice on how to have a successful career. The old gentleman replied, "You got to learn how to make good decisions."

In a follow-up question, the young man said, "Well, how do I learn to make good decisions?"

Without hesitation, the older man replied, "You learn from making bad decisions."

As simple as it may sound, the process of trial and error is a very important part of growth and change for any individual. Making decisions is not an easy thing for a lot of people, especially when the decisions involve change. It's just human nature to become complacent with our lives and not make decisions that will pull us out of our comfort zones.

I have found that many people would rather suffer in silence than make decisions that would alleviate the suffering if that decision involved a life change. I know plenty of people who are in marriages where they just tolerate the other person because they are not willing to decide for change. Some work every day on jobs that they hate. Not because they have to but because they choose to tolerate what they have rather than make decisions that would lead to change.

Making decisions is usually not a hard thing for me, whether they be tough or simple. I am a person who is in touch with my desires, and I have strong likes and dislikes. Add that to my perfectionist tendencies, which often put me in a position where I am constantly forced to make decisions. I almost always know what I want, but I often seek the counsel of others before making a decision just to hear an opposing point of view. Many people have said to me, "I don't know why you are asking for my advice because you are going to do what you want to do no matter what I say."

I agree with that to a certain point. My decisions are almost always a done deal before asking for advice. However, I am not incapable of changing my mind if I am presented with a strong logical reason showing why I should do so. All of my life, I have been making decisions alone and have only come to regret just a few. Most of the time, I have learned to use my bad decisions as a tool of growth to help me make good decisions. That way, I keep myself from repeating the same mistakes.

Transitions

Besides, I usually do not enjoy repeating most things in life over and over again anyway. I am easily bored and always seeking something fresh and new. Although there are a few exceptions to that rule, such as a good meal or a satisfying romantic encounter, which is always worth repeating. However, if I make a decision that brings about bad results, I try to develop a new method to accomplish my goal. Because I find it foolish to do the same thing over and over again and expect a different result.

I have made more important and difficult decisions in life than I can remember. However, I was somewhere in my late fifties when my decision-making ability suddenly began to change. For more than five decades, it had been simply yes or no, left or right, and black or white. Now, I was noticing that I struggled to see the line of definition between my choices. A few times, because of indecisiveness, I would just go with my feelings instead of logic, but I quickly found out that your feelings can lead you to make some bad choices. I would weigh the options and examine the possible outcomes, and I still found it extremely difficult sometimes to make even the most routine decisions. This sudden onset of indecisiveness not only affected my professional life but permeated every part of my personal life.

Some examples of my indecisiveness are that I would buy an airline ticket for vacation and then have difficulty trying to decide whether or not to use it. I would go to a take-out restaurant and end up ordering a couple of different meals because I couldn't decide which one I really wanted. To a lot of people, this may sound like a very simple problem, but the effects of my indecisiveness started causing some really big problems.

Along with the indecisiveness, I began to develop an issue with short-term memory loss. Much more than what was common for my age. It wasn't long before the changes to my cognitive skills were very noticeable to people around me, making me appear somewhat senile at an early age. I found myself shying away from things that were a part of my daily responsibilities because I was afraid of being embarrassed by others seeing that dysfunction in me. I would avoid certain interactions that would challenge my memory. I did not know what to do about these problems and was reluctant to seek help. At the time, I attributed them to the aging process and concluded that it was something I just needed to get used to.

Being an analytical problem solver by nature, I came up with a solution to the indecisiveness and the memory problem. The answer was to write everything down, and if it involved something that I might be questioned on, I would also write down answers. That way, I could review every possible answer and try to decide before being questioned about it. Of course, the downside to this was that I had notes everywhere. I had to research and think through every possible answer, even if that answer would never be used as a solution. This took a tremendous amount of time and caused me a lot of stress.

At this point, I had been taking sleeping medication for years. I was now experiencing insomnia at its worst. It was impossible for me to sleep without medication, and many nights, even with the medication, sleep would completely elude me. I had heard people say that a lack of sleep would leave them feeling like a zombie the next day. I now understood what the zombie effect was like, and I went through it day after day.

I sat in meetings totally zoned out, and when I had to speak, I would ramble and veer so far off course that even I couldn't understand the point I was trying to make. Whenever possible, I would try to keep my responses to a simple yes or no to keep others from noticing my brain fog. Some days, I would zone out while driving. Thank goodness I wasn't reckless, but my mind would sometimes go blank. I would drive right by my exit on the highway, and it would be miles later before I would realize that I was heading in the wrong direction.

I came to realize that what I was suffering from was a combination of sleep deprivation and burnout. After all, I had been struggling with insomnia, holding down two full-time jobs for almost 25 years and driving over 50,000 miles a year. I had been warned for almost a decade by medical professionals that I was pushing the envelope with stress and exhaustion. I was advised to at least let go of one of my positions before

Transitions

I crashed and burned. However, like most people, I saw myself as invincible and kept finding excuses for why I could not let go.

There was always some very important project coming up or something that needed to be done. I put my needs aside to make sure that those projects were successful.

My insomnia problem was now in full gear. Many mornings, I would be up before sunrise and go to work an hour or two early. Because of the early hours, the traffic was usually light, which allowed me to meditate and pray on my way while driving to work. This did not replace my regular prayer time, but it gave me some extra time to meditate, which is something I did often while driving. One cool fall morning, I had packed myself a toasted bagel and a thermos of hot tea to take to the office for breakfast. Walking into the building was always so peaceful that time of morning because I was usually alone at the office. It would allow me some time to plan my day.

Until that morning, I would usually get to my office, drop the briefcase to the floor, sit down and say a short prayer, turn on the computer, and then open my breakfast. However, this particular day, I dropped the briefcase to the floor and just stood there looking around the room as if it were a strange place. I found myself zoning out again as if I were daydreaming while standing up in the middle of the office floor. My mind was blank, and my body seemed paralyzed and unable to move. I could feel my breathing rate increasing, and then a feeling of heaviness came over me. I felt a tear come rolling down my cheek, and then another, and then another. Suddenly, I realized that I was crying and had no idea why I was crying. This episode lasted about five minutes before I could sit down and compose myself.

Although the tears had stopped flowing, the heaviness stayed with me the entire day. All day long, I was in a fog and kept questioning myself about the episode and why I was experiencing such heaviness in my spirit. "Am I having a nervous breakdown?" I thought. "Maybe I'm tired and need a vacation." Never mind that I was already taking about six vacations a year. It came to me that perhaps it was time to let go of that position and transition into the next phase of life. It was not something that I wanted to do, but the signs were there, and it appeared that there was no getting around it. I had heard people say that when it is time for you to go, you will know it. Well, now the time had actually come for me, and I knew it.

Over the next few weeks, I noticed something different about my work experience. There were no more tears, but the heaviness would come and go sporadically, leaving me with a desire to get away from the office. I had nowhere in particular to go; I just needed to get away. Sometimes, I would just get in my car and ride for an hour or two before heading home with some takeout food. It seemed like suddenly, the career that I had enjoyed for years had now become a burden. The joy of accomplishment had vanished. I struggled with these emotions, hoping that they would go away, but they never did. I knew that the tears, the heaviness, and the lack of joy were all clear indicators that it was time to step down and let go of my responsibilities.

"I can't do this anymore," I would hear from within myself. "But I can't quit right now!" I would quickly respond in my mind. What about the bills? What about the unfinished work projects? I am too young to retire! These were some of the thoughts that I wrestled with continuously. However, deep down inside, I knew something had permanently changed, and it was time to let go.

I spent the next couple of months floating through work, unable to focus on assignments while wrestling with myself over a decision I knew was inevitable. I had always wanted to retire early, but age fifty seven was a lot earlier than I had anticipated. Many friends and associates worried about what I would do with myself and the extra time. I still had the church to tend to, which was more than enough to keep me busy.

Letting go was a lot tougher than I could have imagined. I signed my resignation, and then I rescinded it. I signed it a second time and held onto it for weeks because I was not confident I was making the right decision. I crunched numbers forward and backward. I reviewed my options over and over, but I was stuck in the valley of indecision.

Transitions

My indecisiveness became such a problem that I had to set aside some time to fast and pray to gain enough strength to turn in my resignation. I was sure that the answer to my prayers was to resign from my position. Although I was confident that resigning from my position was God's will for me, I still found myself with great concerns about my financial future. However, I found comfort in believing that since it was his will that I would not have to face the future without his help.

I think the biggest question that most people ask themselves when retiring is, am I financially prepared? I knew I was not where I wanted to be financially, but I had managed to pay off most bills and put away a decent emergency fund. Because of my position, I had a pretty decent pension allowance. Still, because of my lifestyle, it would take a lot of adjustments to live within my new means. I promised myself to adhere to a strict budget and not create any new bills. However, I quickly found that even if you try to avoid creating new bills, life sometimes has a way of creating them for you.

Suddenly, I found myself faced with one emergency expense after another. Everything from the HVAC system to the refrigerator went on the blink. I continued to go on vacations and purchase things as I had done previously when I was working. I even traded my car that was paid for and ended up with a large monthly car payment. All of this put a big drain on my finances. So, retirement brought a new stress into my life because I had not learned how to budget my finances.

Besides having to worry about finances, I was facing a whole new set of problems. I was plagued by multiple stress-related health issues. I had planned my retirement so carefully, but I found myself unable to adjust my lifestyle. My spending was out of control, creating a financial dilemma for me. I guess the spending was a source of comfort for me since I did not have another vice, such as smoking or drinking. Heaven knows that I needed some kind of stress relief because the church problems were mounting, and a few people there were simply out of control.

Robert C. Morris

I often wondered if I had made the right choice. I had a choice to give up either my secular vocation or the church. Against the advice of many, I chose to give up my secular job to be able to devote my time solely to the church. Now that I was facing some health challenges, there seemed to be a greater resistance to my leadership at the church, especially from a few of the older lay leaders. I could see that this was an effort from Satan to cause me to regret my decision, but I rejected that way of thinking. The way I saw it was that the decision to give up the job was mine alone to make. However, resigning from a pastorate at a church is a decision that God has to make.

I have always been a strong-willed person who would not back down from a challenge. I prided myself on the fact that I possessed great knowledge and would use that knowledge to win arguments or overcome challenges from those who operated from a cantankerous position. I struggled with so many challenges and acts of defiance from those few church leaders that I could feel myself weakening. Even though it was just a few who opposed me at the church, they had an unbreakable alliance. They were able to wreak havoc and block many of the things that I wanted to accomplish.

The most difficult part of seeing this small, divisive faction's foolish and sometimes wicked behavior was that they received little and sometimes no resistance from the majority, who could have nipped their shenanigans right in the bud. Opposition was getting to be a regular expectation for me at every church board meeting and even in the meetings of the general body.

What happened to those people who said they appreciated all of the sacrifices I had made to build the physical and the spiritual organization that they were now enjoying? They had made many promises to do things in return for my years of dedication and hard work. Most of those promises never came to fruition. Thank goodness I had learned never to take stock in the promises of people. At this point, church, for me, had lost a lot of its joy. It was beginning to feel more like a job than a spiritual calling to serve. If we had a good day or a good week, I could be sure that it would soon be followed by some conflict that needed to be addressed or a challenge from those who opposed me. My friends referred to it as putting out fires.

The stress was mounting. It was taking a devastating toll on my physical health. Things on my body began to hurt that I never knew could hurt. The insomnia was so bad that most of the time, the sleeping pills did not work. If I managed to get two to three hours of sleep a night, I would be doing good. The sleep specialist cleared me of sleep apnea and other disorders and gave me a list of things that I could try to promote solid rest, but none of them seemed to help.

I was constantly on the road and one of my biggest fears was that I would fall asleep while driving. Occasionally, I found myself nodding off and falling asleep for a few seconds. Many days, I was in a foggy state and zoned out from what was being said or done around me at church. And yet, at night, I was constantly recalling things from the day and trying to solve the issues with seemingly no ability to turn off my mind in order to rest.

One morning in the shower, I noticed something that just didn't feel right. There was a hard lump under the skin of my left nipple about the size of a green pea. What is this? I thought. I did not know what it was, but the thought of cancer was in the back of my mind. I am battling insomnia, hypertension, high cholesterol, IBS, acid reflux, asthma, severe allergies, and an arrhythmia. I don't think that I can deal with another problem. I am just falling apart. Is this how I am going out? So many thoughts were running through my mind. I did nothing about it for weeks, thinking that if I just ignored it, it might go away.

Weeks later, it was still there, so I finally decided to seek medical advice. I made an appointment with my doctor and showed him the lump. He examined it and said, "First, you need to have a mammogram, and we can schedule that for this afternoon. Once you get the report, you should take it to a surgeon and have him or her consider removing the lump. The only way to be sure of whether or not it is malignant is to remove it and have it examined by a lab."

Robert C. Morris

This was not what I wanted to hear, but somehow I remained calm. I guess I was so used to being sick at that point that I was just numb to the possibilities. Being male, I never thought I would ever need a mammogram. It was a very uncomfortable and somewhat painful procedure. I was thinking, how do women go through this year after year? I was told that the exam is even more uncomfortable for men because they generally have less breast tissue. When the machine flattens the breast for the scan, it pinches tighter than it does for women. Once the test was complete, the next few days seemed like an eternity waiting for the results.

Unremarkable? How can it be unremarkable? I kept asking myself about the radiology report. It was pretty clear that there was something there. It's not buried in some mass of tissue, but it's right up front where it can be seen and felt. I was bewildered by the radiology report. It seemed like all of my life, my medical conditions were not easily diagnosed or treated.

There was always an inconclusive test or a certain symptom that had not been seen before that would hinder a simple diagnosis or treatment. I quickly made an appointment with a surgeon, hoping that he could provide me with more information.

The surgeon said, "Well, I have good news, and I have bad news. The good news is that I can easily remove it. The bad news is that because of the coding on your referral, the procedure would fall under cosmetic surgery, and your insurance will not cover the costs."

"Okay, I'll let you know what I decide to do," I said. Once again, I was put in a position requiring much thought and prayer before taking the next step. Fortunately, I had the resources to cover the surgery, but what about post-surgery treatments and follow-ups? What happens if the tumor is malignant and I need further treatment? Will I have to pay for that also? I just didn't know what to do.

I have always been the type of person who would speak openly about my illnesses and problems. So, I would sometimes speak in church about my dilemma with this tumor. People would often tell me that they were

Transitions

praying for me and share a story about some similar situation that they or someone they knew was going through. Hearing their stories should have encouraged me. However, it had just the opposite effect. It caused me to become overwhelmed about my condition. It was as if an evil spirit had influenced my thinking and caused me to believe that this was the end of the road for me, and boy, did I swallow that lie hook, line, and sinker.

The combination of health challenges and the constant schisms at the church was stressful and weighed on me heavily. It was easy for many of the parishioners to see from my countenance that I was in a deeply troubled state of mind. One Wednesday night at prayer meeting service, I was sitting in the back pew observing when two of the younger Deacons quietly approached me and asked if they could speak with me privately. Once we were alone in a private room, they expressed how concerned they were about my condition. They asked if they could pray with me and for me. I said okay, but the strange thing is that as much as I believed in the power of prayer, I did not feel like praying at all that night. However, I must admit that their earnest yet simple prayer did make me feel a little lighter.

That Friday, I was able to get the doctor to write out a new referral with a different probable diagnosis code in hopes that the insurance company would not contest it. Once it was accepted under a new code, I could then have the surgery and any possible follow-up care covered by my insurance.

However, I got a big surprise on that Saturday morning. While examining myself, I noticed that the lump was very difficult to find. And when I located it, I found that it was no longer the size of a pea but as small as a BB. And over the next few days, it shrunk to the size of an ant, and then a grain of salt, and then it was completely gone! I searched for a couple of days, thinking that I had missed it or that it would come back. Yet, all the time, I suspected that I had been a recipient of yet another miracle. It was that prayer on Wednesday evening, I said to myself. There was no other explanation for it. I couldn't wait to show the doctor and especially those two Deacons who had prayed for my healing. I am a really blessed individual.

Despite that blessing, the health challenges kept on coming. I would get an upper respiratory infection about once every other month. My vision was changing quickly, and I received a glaucoma diagnosis followed by a Prediabetes diagnosis. This all meant a change of lifestyle as well as more preventive care to keep those conditions from worsening. It seemed as if I was on a perpetual schedule of weekly doctor visits. There were so many medications that there was literally some pill that had to be taken every hour of the day. Nineteen pills a day, not including vitamins and supplements, was not only difficult to remember but made me question if I would ever get any better.

Like many others, I would start a new diet and then fall off the wagon a few weeks later. I was told that sticking to a strict diet was one of the keys to managing some of my physical ailments. I probably would have been more motivated to adhere to a diet plan if my goal was to lose weight, but I never had an obesity problem. I started a home exercise program. I found that daily cardio exercise not only stabilized my weight but it also helped to control the progression of my glaucoma, hypertension, and prediabetes. I still had to be monitored routinely but did not require additional medications to treat those conditions.

Then, a new and strange thing began to happen. I began to fall a lot. Sometimes, I would trip over things; other times, I would just trip over my own feet. Many of the falls would happen in the middle of the night as I attempted to get up and go to the bathroom. It was definitely a balance problem, and it caused me quite a few injuries, some requiring medical attention. I found myself extremely concerned over where all this was heading. Am I aging at warp speed? Am I going to lose my independence? Am I ever going to be free of these ailments? I believe that things can change, but I am almost sixty years old and going downhill quickly. I don't know how much longer I can continue to serve as a Pastor while going through so many physical trials. Especially since I had to face grueling traffic jams and often skipped meals while making a one

Transitions

hundred and thirty mile round trip with each visit to the church. It appeared that only another miracle would be able to change the trajectory of what seemed to be a collision course with disaster.

Week after week, month after month, I struggled to do my job while getting weaker and watching my mind become more and more unfocused. The foggy state of mind I dwelt in plagued me almost twenty four hours a day. It was like I was standing outside myself, watching myself live and work in a slow-motion mode. If someone asked me a question, I sometimes had to repeat it inside my head, maybe a couple of times before I could comprehend it enough to answer. Despite this challenge, I became complacent with my condition. It was more important in my mind for me to meet my obligations than to focus on my condition.

I refused to seek more counseling on what to do because almost everyone I consulted, including my physician, told me that the remedy was to retire and allow myself to rest. To me, that just wasn't an option. Besides, I wasn't really sure how someone retires from pastoral ministry. The work had become my life and was consuming me, but trying to imagine life without it was not something that I could conceive.

BOOM! I had only taken my focus off the road for a second, and the next thing I knew, I had rear-ended another car. I was looking straight ahead, but my mind and reflexes were dull. It was sleeting outside, and by the time I noticed that the car in front of me had stopped, it was too late. I hit the brakes, but the car slid on the slippery road and plowed into the back of the car in front of me. "Oh crap, I am due at the church shortly to give a eulogy. Now, what am I gonna do?" I thought to myself.

The guy in the other car gets out cussing and fussing. He then begins to lecture me on how I should slow down in bad weather. After telling him I had called the police and taken a few pictures with my phone, I returned to my car and rolled up the windows. I needed to get away from him before his belligerence caused me to respond to him in a harsh manner. I called a pastor friend to see if he could fill in for me at the funeral. I had no doubt that I would be tied up with that situation for a while and was feeling nervous about driving any more that day.

After the police made their report, I went home with an empty feeling because I had never had an emergency that caused me to miss an entire service before. This was the second time I had rear-ended another car in a little over a year. The first time was on a Sunday morning. I had zoned out in clear, dry weather and totaled the car that I was driving. I hit my head but refused medical treatment and still made my way to the church. My nephew, who is an ordained minister, had agreed to fill in for me and was just getting ready to deliver his sermon when I arrived. It was after the second accident that something unusual started happening. I began to lose the desire to get on the road to drive to the church. I had become nervous and somewhat frightened about being on the highway, especially during rush hour. I would often have to push myself to get behind the wheel. It was suddenly becoming clear in my mind that I needed to seriously consider a sabbatical or retiring.

I decided that I needed to speak with the church again about a transitional retirement plan. I knew that I would not be able to just leave on my own, but if I could get the ball rolling and help them find a replacement, it would force me to let go. Besides, a pastoral transition is a very successful method used by many churches to eliminate being without a pastor and the adverse effects of having the position vacant. I firmly believed that because we had a mortgage and a waning congregation that this approach would definitely be the best way to deal with a leadership change.

The meeting went very poorly, with many not understanding my reason for wanting to retire. "How can we choose another pastor with you sitting right here? I can't do that!" said one woman who I considered a personal friend. "I don't think you should be hand-picking the next pastor. If you are gonna leave, then do that. We'll be okay," said one of the officers in a belligerent tone.

"Wow," I thought to myself. "After almost three decades of service, nobody was expressing any concern about me or the reason why I

Transitions

wanted to retire." All I was hearing was selfish anger and a negative reaction to my announcement. I went home that day bewildered by their reaction. I thought maybe they did not believe that I was serious about leaving, but in my heart, I knew that it was inevitable.

It was the Sunday before Christmas, and one of the choirs sponsored a family and friends fellowship service at the church that afternoon. I had not been feeling the greatest, but I managed to smile my way through the day. I had been struggling for about six weeks with what I thought was a urinary tract infection. I was taking a prescription medication and cranberry juice to treat it. When I arrived home, I had a strong urge to urinate and a burning sensation afterward. It appeared that my condition was worsening. I grabbed the medication and went to the refrigerator for some cranberry juice. As I opened the refrigerator door, I noticed my hand shaking uncontrollably. And within a few seconds, my whole body was shaking, and my legs began to get wobbly.

Suddenly, I felt so cold that it was like I was standing in a snowstorm at the North Pole with no clothes on. "Oh my gosh, why is my whole body shivering? Do I have the flu?" were the last words I remember thinking before I felt my knees hitting the floor.

I was so weak that I could not get up off the floor, so I crawled from the kitchen and up a flight of stairs to the bedroom. The heat was on in the house, but I felt like an icicle inside. I was so cold that my body began to shiver so hard that my teeth chattered. I turned the space heater on high in the bedroom, hoping to warm up, and wrapped myself in blankets. "I must have the flu. Should I call someone to come and help me?" So many thoughts were running quickly through my head.

Suddenly, I had an urge to urinate as if someone had my bladder in their hand and was squeezing it like a sponge.

However, when I tried to relieve myself, nothing came out. I began to experience pains that, if measured on a scale of one through ten, would be an eleven. The pain again brought me to my knees, with tears rolling down my face. I wailed with a screech of torment, breathing heavily through my mouth.

Robert C. Morris

In desperation, I decided to call a friend to discuss the situation. "It doesn't appear that it is life-threatening, but the pain is off the charts," I said in trying to describe my situation.

You need to go to the hospital said the voice on the other end of the phone.

"I hate hospitals and would have to be unconscious and carried out on a stretcher before I would go to one," I replied. So, I decided to take some Tylenol with some cranberry juice and lay there in excruciating pain for the next nine hours.

I did not sleep for more than ten minutes at a time and was up at sunrise seeking out medical attention. Because the pains were in my bladder area and I also could not urinate, my first thought was to call my Urologist. I called and got a recorded message that the number was disconnected. When I looked online, I found out that he had retired. I tried to call another Urologist that I had consulted many years ago, but he had also retired. I decided to call my primary doctor to see who he would recommend, and his office gave me two names. Both were booked and could not schedule an appointment for several weeks. I sat there feeling I had no choice but to go to the hospital.

Lord, help me, I said under my breath. After uttering those words, I looked down at the phone book, which had fallen open to a new page. My eyes made instant contact with a Urology Associates Group about twenty five miles away. I heard a small voice say to me, "Call them." "Okay, it's confirmed, tomorrow at one thirty. Thank you," I said as I hung up the phone. I started packing my overnight bag to take with me just in case I was sent from the doctor's office to the hospital. My pain level led me to believe that this could possibly be something that would require hospitalization and or surgery.

After being asked dozens of questions by his assistant, Doctor Travis walked into the room. He was quite young, probably a few years out of med school, with an excellent bedside manner. He was reading my registration information as he walked into the examination room. He

Transitions

said, "I think I already know what is wrong with you, but please go ahead and tell me your complaint."

After listening to me recall the chain of events, he said, "Okay, the problem is that you have a serious bladder infection that has infected your blood. The pain you feel is because your prostate is swollen and has blocked off your urethra and the flow of urine. It's called BPH Benign Prostatic Hyperplasia. Let me make this clear: it is not cancer. The chills and fever that you are experiencing are your body's reaction to a UTI infection that is now also in your bloodstream. However, I want to say to you again that it is not cancer."

Dr. Travis explained, "The remedy for the infection is an antibiotic and a silodosin medication to relax your prostate so that you can urinate. Because if you retain urine too long, it can be fatal. Also, because the infection is in your bloodstream, the medications should be administered intravenously in a medical facility,"

"Oh no, I can't go to the hospital! I just hate hospitals. Isn't there another way?" I asked.

"Well, only because you caught this just in the nick of time and seem like you will follow directions, I will allow you to try treating this at home. It will require a thirty-day treatment of Cipro™ and a daily dosage of Rapaflo™. You must keep daily records of your progress and be here to see me in one week for a follow-up. Also, the medication must start today, not tomorrow, but today. Agreed?" he said authoritatively.

"Agreed," I responded with great relief.

The medications worked well. I could feel some progress in only a few days, although I realized I was nowhere close to being well. The Cipro™ was tolerable, but the Rapaflo™ had many side effects, including increased insomnia and dry ejaculations. It also killed my libido and, on a scale of one to ten, left it around one. The drastic change in my body worried me quite a bit. It was like everything below the belt had died. I shared my concerns with my primary physician, and he said, "Well, you might need to get used to it because a prostate can enlarge, but it doesn't shrink." Of course, this news did not sit well with me. In just a matter of weeks, I had lost control of my bladder. I felt more sexually defunct than a ninety year old without any hope of change.

During the first two follow-up visits to the urologist, all of my test results were good. Doctor Travis asked, "Any questions?"

"Yes, the Silodosin medication has killed my libido. How long will I have to take that medication?" I asked.

"Probably for the rest of your life," he responded. "But there are remedies for your libido," he said as he handed me a sample box of Cialis™ from the medicine cabinet. This is not only good for erectile dysfunction, but it has worked well for many people in helping to shrink the prostate. Here is a sample packet. Try it out and let me know how it works for you on your next visit."

There was an overwhelming feeling of heaviness within me when I left his office. Taking medication every day for allergies, hypertension, cholesterol, and insomnia was one thing, but now a daily medication just to be able to pee? I turned sixty, and the following month, it seemed like I was falling apart. "Why am I having so many health issues? I take up to nineteen pills a day, yet it appears that my general health is getting worse instead of better. What can I do to help myself before I am either no longer here or in a nursing home somewhere? Lord Jesus, give me wisdom and give me healing!" I cried from within.

I did not want to take the Cialis™, but in obedience, I took it. On the first day, I was fine, but on the second day, I developed a headache of migraine proportion. I had pains in my arms and a few muscle spasms in my legs. I was feeling pretty lousy but did not immediately associate it with the new medication.

On the third day, I had a funeral to attend in another city around noontime. I started to take the Cialis™ after breakfast and then hit the road, but a little voice inside me said not to, so I didn't take it.

It was a sixty-mile trip one way, and I was just about there when a stabbing pain went from my thigh down into my foot. I could no longer use my right foot to drive the car. I had been prone to muscle cramps in

Transitions

the past, but nothing like this. As I veered off the road in tremendous pain, I wondered if I would be able to go any further or have to wait there and call for help. I sat there almost paralyzed by fear and pain. My head was now hurting so bad that it was affecting my vision. After about fifteen minutes, I was able to sit sideways on my right hip and use my left foot to drive the car.

"I made it. There's the church," I said to myself just as a painful muscle spasm hit my side and caused me to bend over sideways. Suddenly, I lost the use of my left foot. I could not hit the brakes and was doubled over in pain. I also found myself unable to steer the car. I felt a jolt and heard a scraping sound, and when I looked up, I saw that my car sideswiping every vehicle on the right side of this narrow street. "Oh God, I'm gonna die," I thought. But out of nowhere came a sudden surge of strength, and through the pain, I stomped the brakes, thus stopping the car. I later discovered that I was allergic to Cialis™ and had a severe allergic reaction that day. I dread to think what would have happened if I had not listened to that little voice inside of me and had taken another pill right before getting on the road.

The thirty-day antibiotic treatment period was an extremely difficult time to get through. I would stay in bed resting most of the week just to have enough strength to attend church on Sunday. Through all the physical challenges, I still never missed a Sunday serving in church. My sense of dedication told me that I just had to be there despite the advice of many parishioners who told me I should stay home and rest. After weeks of forced rest and watching my body recover, it became apparent to me that an extended period of rest was the only solution to repairing my deteriorating health if I was ever going to get any better. I prayed for guidance for several weeks before taking the next step on what I thought would be a journey to recovery.

I called together some of the leaders of the Diaconate Ministry to discuss my fleeting health and the possibility of taking a sabbatical. "Maybe three to six months without pay," I suggested. I was surprised by the selfish responses that I received. "That would be so bad for the church," one man said. "You think we have financial problems now," said another. Every response dealt with how my absence would affect the church, with no concern for how my life would be affected without taking a leave. I did not know where all this was going, but I felt that another turning point or transition was on the horizon for my life. I prayed daily for something to change so that I might be able to get the necessary retreat before I suffered from some irreversible debilitating illness. Because of my condition, I was often zoned out to most things around me. I found myself going through the motions of serving, but the true joy and desire for shepherding were slowly fading away from me. When I first noticed the joy of service waning, I thought it was just a symptom of my exhaustion and that the joy would eventually return, but it didn't. I still had tremendous love and compassion for those that I served. However, a noticeable tiredness overshadowed me like a man who had just run a marathon race.

Looking back, I realize that life is so designed that when you neglect to make necessary changes, life will often step in and make them for you. And sometimes, when you pray for a solution to a problem, the answer to your prayer takes you on a journey that will lead you into a place of transition. We always want answers to fix our circumstances without interrupting our so-called norm. However, when we fail to move into the next phase of life voluntarily, many times, the hand of God will usher us into it despite our unwillingness to change. For me, this is exactly what happened.

One Sunday morning, as my family and I got out of the car to enter the church, I noticed two deacons standing at the door waiting to assist me with my shoulder bag and vestments. They did this faithfully with a smile, and I always looked forward to their greeting as well as their assistance.

As we entered the rear door of the church, I heard a whispering voice behind me say, "Getttt outttt!."

Transitions

"Did you hear that?" I would ask as I turned to see if someone was behind me. I thought that perhaps someone was hiding near the door playing a game, but no one else was around.

"Hear what?" the Deacons would respond. I am sure those Deacons probably thought I was going coo-coo, but it was not my imagination.

After it happened a few times, it occurred to me that perhaps some kind of evil spirit was taunting me because it would happen almost every Sunday. To this day, I cannot be sure whether it was something evil or not that whispered those words, but I know without a doubt that it was some kind of spiritual presence. Was this a warning of some kind, or was this a threat? The only thing I could be sure of was that I was the only one who heard it.

As I grew physically weaker, I could feel myself also getting more mentally confused. There were many times that I would start a sentence and then lose my train of thought before I could finish it. I would constantly make notes, even about the simplest of matters, because I would forget things I was told moments earlier. As troubled as I was by these developments, I attributed them mainly to the aging process and continued to focus on my work responsibilities instead of my own physical health and mental well-being.

I continued to pray for a solution to improve my health while at the same time pushing myself to the limit. I did this primarily because I am a perfectionist who believes that if I cannot find a solution, then perhaps there is none to be found. I am the same way with projects. I will review and try to improve them until I believe it is essentially perfect and I am totally exhausted. Tenacity should have been my middle name because giving up or mediocrity is not an option for me.

One morning at about 3:00 a.m. I woke up startled by a night terror. My heart was pounding so hard that I could hear every beat in my ears. I was drenched with sweat and hyperventilating. My first thought was that I had to get up and change my night clothes. These night terrors happened so often that I had developed a routine reaction. Get up, change your clothes, use the bathroom, and take another sleeping pill. It was the only way that I could usually get back to sleep.

As I'm changing my clothes, I hear the sound of a creaking floor, like someone walking around on the first floor of my home. "How could someone get inside my house without setting off the alarm?" Should I call 911?" I thought to myself. I sat on the edge of the bed, terrified, trying to decide what to do. And then the creaking stopped just as quickly as it had started. However, a thorough check of the premises revealed that there was no one in the entire house except for me.

About a week later, after sleeping for only about two hours, I woke up again, startled by yet another nightmare. It had unnerved me so badly that I had to sit up on the side of the bed to calm myself. As I was panting for breath, I had this strange feeling that I was not alone. I felt the presence of someone on my right side. As I turned to look to my right, I caught a glimpse of a man sitting on the bed next to me. He quickly pulled a thick plastic bag over my head and drawstrings the bottom of it around my neck. I struggled to get free, but he had a tight grip on me from behind and was much stronger than me. I felt myself gasping for air and slowly suffocating as the bag was sealed tightly around my neck. Then I heard a loud scream, and I realized it was me as I sat up quickly in the bed.

Suddenly, I realized that I was now awake and all that had just taken place was really a dream, including the man sitting on my bed. I would no longer see these events as just nightmares but started referring to them as night terrors because they were so vivid and terrified me to the core. Many times, it was very difficult for me to separate the dream from reality until after I was awake for a few minutes. I wondered within myself how long this could go on without me having some kind of physical or mental breakdown. There was no doubt in my mind that these occurrences were abnormal. I would pray every day before interacting with the world to be covered with spiritual armour (Ephesians 6) and that my mind be kept in peace (Isaiah 26). I know without a doubt that only prayer brought me through this period of what seemed like a path to insanity.

Transitions

"Why do you keep getting so many infections? You do realize that you are falling apart?" My primary physician said while I was on his examination table. "Your blood pressure is out of control. Your A1C is steadily rising. Your cholesterol is too high. Your COPD is getting worse. Your arteries are showing signs of calcification. Your IBS is chronic. You have developed glaucoma. You have recurring pressure sores, and you are an insomniac. All of these things, in my opinion, are exacerbated by stress. When are you going to retire? They can get somebody else to do what you do!" He spoke to me sharply, like a big brother or father.

"Soon" was all that I replied. I left his office and drove down the highway with tears rolling down my cheeks. I knew that I was mentally and physically exhausted and pushing it to the limit with my health. However, giving up would be quitting, and I have never been a quitter. I saw the signs of my condition almost daily and chose to adapt to them rather than act upon them. I was so sleep-deprived and mentally drained that, many days, I would slump over and fall asleep at the dinner table with the fork in my hand.

There were days when I would pull into my garage and sit in the car for thirty minutes because I did not have the strength to get out of the car and walk into the house. It was not unusual after dinner for me to crawl up the stairs on my hands and knees to get to my bedroom. However, giving up just did not seem like an option to me.

One Sunday, as I was dropping off family members after church, my niece walked out of the house and jumped into the car with me. She asked me how I was feeling. I was honest with her about my exhaustion and physical ailments. Then she blurted out, "So, when are you going to retire? I don't like what I see going on with you. It will be interesting to see in a year's time how many of these ailments you might not have anymore."

All I could say to her was "soon." I wanted to break down and cry at that moment because the truth really sunk in. I knew that I was heading for a time of transition. I also knew I really did not want to go through that transition because I was afraid of change and the unknown.

I sought prayer and counseling from several pastors in my close circle for guidance on what I was considering. I was candid and open about every detail of my situation. After hearing my circumstances all of them except for one agreed that I needed to step down from my position. It was not what I wanted to hear, but I knew deep inside that it would be the right decision. I spent weeks wrestling in prayer, trying to decide when and how to take the next step. I knew my decision would not be any easier for the church than it was for me. However, I was hoping that there might be some meeting of the minds and a solution would be found where I would not have to totally absolve myself of the position.

It was midday one Saturday, and I was praying and meditating and putting the finishing touches on Sunday's sermon. I had an overwhelming urge to just sit still and stare at the wall when suddenly a figure appeared next to the wall, which I believe was a messenger angel. Initially, he said nothing but just looked at me with a piercing, steady stare. Suddenly, I was lifted from my seat and floated upward into a space that was bright and had no boundaries. And like the Apostle Paul said in 2nd Corinthians chapter 12, whether I was in the body or out, I could not tell. I heard a voice speaking in an unknown tongue, and I soon realized that the voice I was hearing was my own.

Words cannot express the sense of security, freedom, and overwhelming joy that I experienced at that moment. I am not sure how long this experience lasted because any sense of time had left me. It might have only been a few minutes, but I did not care if it had lasted forever because I was filled with such peace. Then, with the same speed I had ascended, I descended back to where I had been sitting. This angelic being was still there, standing before me and speaking to my mind in a method similar to telepathy. He said only three words: "You are released," and then he disappeared in the same manner he had appeared.

I must have wept for the next hour because this experience not only strengthened my faith but also taught me some lessons that I will

Transitions

remember for the rest of my life. The first lesson that I learned was that when God speaks to you personally, he is clear and unmistakable in his message. It was not the answer to my prayers that I wanted, but there was no mistaking of what was said. Number two, my assignment was not my choice, but it was God's choice for me. Just as he can assign, he can also withdraw that assignment, and my job was simply to be obedient and follow his direction. Transition time had come, and it was time to move on to my next assignment, although I had no idea what that mission would be. Number three, God is real and very much involved in the lives of his servants. This event erased any doubts that I might have previously had about God's lack of involvement in every aspect of my life.

For several years, I had sought a solution to my situation. I had hoped that the answer would be different from the one that I received, but it wasn't. It appeared that the answer only came after I made my prayers a personal request for help. I had been praying and requesting help for "us" and not for "me." I came to see that although the people I served were connected to me spiritually, the ministry assignment from God was mine alone. Each divine assignment is personal and specific to the individual. In other words, my assignment is mine, and your assignment is yours. Also, every assignment comes with a mission, a time frame, and a purpose.

Shortly after this experience, I sat quietly in my office, staring at the keyboard of my computer. Reluctantly, I began typing as I felt the tears rolling down my face. I wrote three different letters of resignation with varying dates of resignation. I placed them in a folder for the church meeting the following Saturday. In some weird way, choosing three dates helped me feel better about what I was doing. Two of the dates were so far in the future that I thought it would give me an opportunity to work something out instead of actually resigning. I had thought many times before what retiring or leaving would actually be like, but nothing could have prepared me for the emotional stress that a life-changing decision like that could cause. Now that it was time to go, I did not want to leave, but my health issues had me afraid that I might die if I stayed. I thought about trying again to make a sabbatical deal, but now I had received directions from God. How do I defy his decision? I wanted to submit the letter with the most extended date, but every adviser said to me that it would not be wise because these kinds of things can sometimes become contentious.

At the meeting the next Saturday I was feeling very ill and tired. I sat and watched as some people debated over petty issues. Others even became belligerent in their attitudes towards each other. As I reached into my folder to grab a letter, I was moved to submit the one with the shortest notice, seven weeks. I interrupted the meeting ruckus to state that I had a very important announcement to make. "I would like to offer a letter of resignation," I stated. There was a sudden and uncanny silence in the room for about thirty seconds. The silence was only broken by the church Clerk, who volunteered to read the letter out loud to the membership.

After the Clerk finished reading, there was again a strange and uncanny silence in the room. No one even asked a single question. A couple of people were so upset that you could see tears welling up in their eyes. What had I done? Was this the right time? Can't they see that I had no other option? These were just a few of the many thoughts running through my mind at that moment. It was very obvious that the shock of the announcement had left everyone speechless, so I decided to have a time of prayer and close out the meeting.

People left that afternoon without even saying goodbye, and I could feel the anger brewing up in so many. They were now faced with the reality of something that I had been talking with them about for three years. Despite the forewarning, they were still caught off-guard because they had not seen or understood the seriousness of my personal circumstances. If I had been in a hospital bed or shut-in at home, that would have probably been understandable. However, most people only saw what they chose to see and never heard a word I said about why I was led to resign. Of course, a few secretly applauded my departure because of their own selfish desire for power and control. Those people did not waste any time setting their plans into motion. However, I could not worry about that now. I had finally done what was best for me and had to keep moving forward.

Returning to the church the next morning for service was like going to a totally strange place. The environment was void of joy, and many people totally avoided me out of hurt and anger. It was like being ostracized in the very place that I had served for thirty years. It was very difficult to imagine how I would desire to even come back the following week, but I did.

I had a meeting with the deacon chairman and told him that I would like to meet with the church board to discuss some departure issues. He said, "I don't think they want to meet with you." I did not know at the time that a few of the board members had called a secret meeting among themselves to discuss my resignation. They expressed their anger to each other and decided to send me a certified letter accepting my resignation without ever getting the approval of the church membership. This annoyed me greatly, and I could have easily made them rescind it, but I thought to myself that fighting that battle was not worth the stress. Besides, I had been given instructions by God, and challenging a letter would not change the outcome. I knew the letter was motivated by the advice of some power-hungry individuals who preyed on the ignorance and emotions of those who didn't know any better.

I was in week three of seven, and I called a meeting of the entire church on a Saturday afternoon to discuss my departure. More people were there than I had seen in church for many years. I explained my situation and opened my heart to them, which seemed well accepted. However, whenever I was asked a question about possibly staying a little longer, a certain deacon would interrupt and try to answer for me. He clearly showed me that he did not want that possibility to be discussed.

He also knew that he and several others had secretly mailed an unauthorized letter accepting my resignation. If there was a reversal of my decision or that letter was revealed, it would present a serious problem for him and his group of cronies.

At the time of the meeting, I had not yet received the letter, and it was not mentioned to me or the church body that day that it had been sent. After the meeting, several members came to me to express their regrets over my leaving. One older woman said to me, "You know, I'm really gonna miss you. However, I don't blame you for leaving because your church board ain't sh**! Oops, excuse me, Pastor, but they ain't!" We both smiled as we exchanged a hug.

The next few weeks were tormenting, and they tried every fiber of my being. Many shunned me, and some were non-responsive to anything I requested of them, even if it was a part of their regular duties. I spoke with a couple of my advisers about the attitude of some of the people and how I just wanted to leave immediately and not wait out my last two weeks. One told me, "The problem is that this has turned contentious, and you just have to pray your way through it." Another said, "Wow, with all that you have done for them! However, you must be above all this and keep your word. You only have a couple more weeks." I knew they were right in my heart, but it was hard to keep the righteous indignation I felt inside from causing me to lash out.

My last Sunday morning as pastor was a lot harder than I had anticipated. People had come from other churches to hear my farewell message. Many members of my family, as well as ministers from other churches, came to show their support. The Spirit of God had given me a prophetic message that I did not enjoy preaching. Primarily because it contained spiritual warnings about seasons of change that were on its way for that particular congregation. I called everyone together at the close of service to pray together. I asked God's blessing upon the people and released them into the hands of God.

A few very kind people set up some tables in the dining hall with refreshments. Some local pastors stopped by to wish me well. Yet half of the people that I served for over thirty years would not even stop to shake my hand or say goodbye. When the day was over, I had to work

Transitions

through some feelings of bitterness that were developing inside of me. I needed to understand how people who come to church in the name of Christ and profess to be Christians could be so hardhearted and callous. The separation was just as difficult for me as it was for them. It would not have taken very much for them to convince me to stay a while longer, but anger over my decision seemed to guide their actions. However, God showed me at a later date why he had allowed them to harden their hearts. He did it so I would not change my mind; it was transition time, and he had other work for me to do.

The next few months presented a time of great challenge for me. There is an old saying that many pastors allow their title to define them. I do not believe I had let the title define me, but there was definitely a strange emptiness inside me. I was unable to see a transitional pathway that I could take in order to move forward. I felt that suddenly, I was out in the wilderness without a compass. This was so different for me because I had always had a goal, path, and direction right before me. I would always work hard, sometimes too hard, toward those goals with great tenacity until they were accomplished. Suddenly, I found myself in the valley of "NOW WHAT?" Serving the church was all I knew; it was my life purpose. Week after week, I felt a void on Sunday because I had been preaching for almost forty years. Now, I was sitting silent, listening to someone else. Yet, I knew I still had a whole lot of preaching and teaching left inside of me.

Probably one of the most difficult things I had to deal with in the post-pastoral period was the sudden cut-off of communication with other pastors I had been in touch with regularly for many years. It was pretty obvious from their actions that their friendships were superficial and based upon quid quo pro activities. Many of them had said to me in the weeks prior to my retirement that they would keep in touch and would invite me to come and preach for them one Sunday. I did not ask for this favor, but it was offered to me without solicitation. Sadly, once I actually left the pastoral ministry, I never heard from most of them again, and some of them would not even return my calls. It had always been a desire of mine to one day evangelize, but I could not even see that coming to pass because the very people I depended on to provide some opportunity had forsaken me. While praying one day, I heard a voice whisper to me, "Sit still for three months." I had heard this voice before. I knew it was a divine whisper, so I was determined in my heart to be obedient.

The following three months were in the dead of winter, and the weather outside was atrocious. It seemed like the ice and snowstorms only came on the weekends, and since I didn't drive in inclement weather, it forced me to stay home on most Sundays. I began to understand that this period was to help deprogram and transition me into the next phase of my journey. The first goal was to focus on learning how to rest and improving my physical health. I noticed a change in my blood pressure and sleeping patterns after just a couple of months. After fourteen years of chronic insomnia, I sometimes fell asleep early at night and slept for hours.

At the end of the three-month period, I started to visit those churches that I was familiar with and had an established relationship with the pastor. The reception was warm, and everyone extended an invitation for me to come and minister to them. Strangely enough, invitations started coming in from churches that I had never been to before. God was opening new doors for me with people that I hardly knew. Most of my invitations came because of word of mouth. If someone had attended one of my services, they would recommend me as a guest somewhere else. Suddenly, I found that my calendar was full. I did not expect or want that many obligations, but I had never been a person who knew how to say no. Also, I love preaching and teaching the Gospel, and it was through serving others that I was beginning to heal. I could feel a change on the horizon.

In all ways acknowledge him, and he shall direct your path.
Proverbs 3:6

Chapter Twelve

TRANSFORMATION

Despite seeing that my life was moving in a new direction, I still often found myself in post-pastoral retirement, searching for answers to my new purpose in life. I believe that I was searching because change is so difficult for me. I felt lost without a clear vision for the future. In my mind, everyone has a purpose. We may not know or fully understand our purpose, but everybody has one. I had always felt that my purpose was pastoral ministry. Now that door was closed. I felt strange, as if I was in the middle of nowhere without any direction on which way to turn. It was as if I had jumped into a spaceship and landed on another planet. Nothing seemed familiar to me anymore, and nothing was satisfying me spiritually. A serious thirst for the things of the past was growing inside me. I felt insecure not being in my comfort zone where things were familiar to me. I reached a point where I wanted to totally detach myself from anything related to church and go into seclusion.

It was a very difficult and confusing transitional period, but I learned its most important lesson. The lesson is that life is a series of transitions that we can only move through successfully when we are prepared to step out of our comfort zone and move forward in order to grow. The

Robert C. Morris

Apostle Paul put it best when he said, "We must forget those things which are behind and reach forth unto those things which are before (Philippians 3:13). I heard a wise person once say that a comfort zone is a beautiful place but nothing ever grows there. Moving out of your comfort zone can be painful, it can be confusing, and sometimes lonely, but the benefits of change can sometimes be invaluable. It is not the lesson's responsibility to teach us but our own responsibility to learn from the lesson and grow.

For me, growing can be extremely difficult because I am a very habitual person by nature. I tend to get stuck in the groove of a comfort zone and stay there until something comes along to force me out of it. Here I was in my senior years of life with no vision, no comfort zone, no feeling of purpose, and no idea of which way to turn. All this was complicated by the increasing bitterness I felt toward those who had been mean and acted angrily toward me when I decided that I needed change. For quite some time, I would carry this resentment because I could not understand their actions or understand that they were just simply being human. I guess I had a lot to learn about human nature. Besides, it wasn't the majority, but only a few people.

During this transitional period, it was hard for me to see my own faults because I had prided myself on dotting every "I" and crossing every "T". So, I felt as though I had done nothing wrong. Therefore, the treatment that I was receiving was very unjust. However, even if my assessment of the situation was correct, It was a teaching moment that taught me that I still had a lot to learn about life and people. I could not grow until I first dealt with myself and got free of all the emotional baggage keeping me from moving forward.

Some wise person once said that real freedom is when you take control over how anybody or anything outside of yourself will affect you. So, it was important for me to learn how to see things in a way that was beneficial to my own well-being. I had to learn how to determine if a situation or an action was really important enough for me to care about it. I had lived in a predominantly reactive state of mind all my life. Now,

Transitions

I had to learn not only how to be proactive but also how to decide whether or not to allow myself to care enough to let something affect me. This was all part of a growing process that would facilitate my transformation.

The amazing part about this particular transformation was that the more I uncluttered my mind, the lighter I felt. The lighter I felt, the more I began to grow with new thoughts, new experiences, and new revelations that began to fill those old spaces. I have come to see that the completion of one's transition in life is the true transformation of one's character and thought process and then putting those thoughts into action. Until your thoughts and actions change, you may be in the process of transition, but your transformation is still incomplete. Whether change comes rapidly or slowly, it is necessary and evidence of transformation.

While meditating and soul-searching, I found that one of the biggest obstacles to my transformation was learning how to truly forgive. True forgiveness was a little more complex than what I had been taught over the years. Learning the art of true forgiveness was no easy accomplishment, and it took me down a path where every time I wanted to deal with a trespass against me, I had to first start with a self-examination. I found that the more I learned to forgive, the less others were able to hurt me. The more I focused on knowing myself, the better I could understand others. When I started seriously practicing these things, I experienced an amazing period of growth both mentally and spiritually. I could actually feel myself growing in knowledge and understanding of things like I had never experienced before. It became clear to me that I was finally changing in preparation for the next season of my life.

Do not misunderstand, transitioning from one season to another is no simple process. Because it requires a willingness to let go of the past and purge yourself of all the things that would hold you from moving forward. There must be time spent in meditation where you take a serious look at yourself and who God is, then seek his purpose for your life. It is not a rushed period that is under your control but a transformation of your inner man that is divinely unfolded unto you in God's own time. Your part is simply to prepare yourself to receive it and then become obedient to your assignment.

The process took a couple of years before I could actually see the new man emerging and catch hold of the vision God had put before me. Once transformed, I started to notice that more people than ever were requesting to meet with me for advice. A lot of them were men and women who were aspiring to Christian Ministry, and many of them were very young people. I have always had a great rapport with young people. However, this new beginning had taken me from simply being a friend to younger people to becoming more of a father figure that they could confide in and trust. I found myself not only giving them Godly counsel but often sharing my life experiences and mentoring them.

Among the many great things that took place during this transformation period was the restoration of my failing health. When I retired from Pastoral Ministry, my health was in such bad shape that I honestly did not believe it would ever get any better. But as I started the period of transformation and became divinely aligned with God's plan for me, I noticed my health also changing for the better.

These were not small changes but major diagnoses that were previously of great concern that began to change. My blood pressure, which was previously difficult to control, was now regulated without any significant spikes. The hemoglobin and diabetes issues had disappeared. After fourteen years of chronic insomnia, I began to sleep every night without any kind of sleeping aid. So many more ailments just simply disappeared. My general health went from a range of about one or two to a really solid ten. It became very clear to me that there is a correlation between spiritual health and physical health.

The restoration of my health brought such peace and happiness into my life that it cannot be fully expressed in words. I had learned the hard way that the two most important things we have in life are our

Transitions

relationship with God and our physical health. I now guard and protect both of them with all of my strength.

I counted my renewed health as a perk from God for being obedient to his instructions and allowing my life to transition into the next phase. Prior to this transition, my vision of retirement was one of resting, traveling, and enjoying new experiences. However, I now believe that in Kingdom work, retirement is another name for a change of course where we simply go from an old assignment to a new one. In this new phase of life, I have found a happiness that eluded me for years. My relationship with God is now closer than it's ever been, and I have a peace that was nowhere to be found in my many previous years of life.

I think the most important change is that I am at peace with myself because I accept myself for who I am and not by what others expect me to be. I no longer see myself through someone else's eyes. I know who I am, and I am who I am. I do not allow myself to be defined by my weaknesses or societal standards but by who God says I am. I have found not only love for myself but how to love others unconditionally. I am no longer confused about how to separate love from lust and now know how to express love in a personal relationship.

What I now see in myself occasionally surprises me. Especially when I am confronted by my own weaknesses and then somehow summon the strength to deal with them. The gift of dreams and visions is still alive and active in my life. I still wrestle with them many times, trying to interpret them and separate the natural realm from the spiritual. However, because of my many previous years of experience with them, I have learned how not to become overwhelmed by them.

When I look back over the years, it becomes clear to me that life is not just a test and preparation for the hereafter but a mission where we struggle from the cradle to the grave to accomplish our assignment. We do not get to choose which obstacles, which adversities, or which roadblocks will confront us. However, we can choose to grow from each experience by how we respond to them. My responses to my struggles in the past ranged from downright pitiful to sometimes pretty good. Yet, in my transformed state, I make much better decisions with little or no regret. This leaves me confident that I am fulfilling my purpose on earth. When this journey is over, I can say, like the Apostle Paul in Second Timothy Chapter 4 Verse 7, "I have fought a good fight, I have finished my course, I have kept the faith."

His lord said unto him, Well done, thou good and faithful servant: thou hast been faithful over a few things, I will make thee ruler over many things: enter thou into the joy of thy lord. Matthew 25:21

About the Author

Reverend Doctor Robert C. Morris is a native of New Jersey. He acknowledged his call to Christian Ministry in November 1980. He was ordained by a Christian Minister's Council of New Jersey and New York in May 1982. He completed undergraduate studies at the Mercer County Community College and The College of New Jersey, where he majored in Business Administration and Marketing. He has received certificates of course completion from the Lockman Bible Institute, the Metropolitan School of Insurance Marketing, and Certified Public Manager Training for the State of New Jersey. He has received certification from Rutgers University of New Jersey for completion of studies in Environmental Law and Regulation. He received his Doctor of Divinity degree from the Bethel Bible College and Seminary in 1999.

He retired after 25 years of service from the New Jersey Department of Environmental Protection, where he served as Manager of the Air Quality Information System and New Facility Registration Office. He was also the Senior Pastor of a Baptist Church in Union County, New Jersey, where he retired after 30 years of service.

Robert C. Morris

Dr. Morris has received proclamations and citations from the United States White House and County and Municipal Government Offices, recognizing his community empowerment work and achievements in Christian Ministry. He currently resides in New Jersey and travels the country evangelizing and preaching the gospel.

Appendix A

This is a photocopy of the mail I received from Lee F. Brown. He was the Public Safety Commissioner of Atlanta, Georgia, serving from 1978 to 1982. Brown and his staff oversaw the investigation of the Atlanta Child Murders case.

Appendix B

This is a photocopy of the letter of thanks from Lee F. Brown.

CITY OF ATLANTA
MAYNARD JACKSON, MAYOR
DEPARTMENT OF PUBLIC SAFETY
175 DECATUR STREET, S.E.
ATLANTA, GEORGIA 30335
(404) 658-7845

LEE P. BROWN
Public Safety Commissioner

Mr. Robert C. Morris
34 Western Avenue, #19
Trenton, New Jersey 08618

Dear Mr. Morris:

I sincerely thank you for contacting the Atlanta Metropolitan Special Task Force on Missing and Murdered Children in reference to the missing and murdered children cases.

If there is any additional information you want to share, please feel free to call the Task Force at (404)658-6818.

Your concern and interest are greatly appreciated.

Sincerely,

Lee P. Brown

LPB:mja

Made in the USA
Coppell, TX
19 July 2024